HAUNTED
ROCKFORD,
ILLINOIS

HAUNTED ROCKFORD, ILLINOIS

KATHI KRESOL
FOREWORD BY DALE KACZMAREK

Haunted
America

Published by Haunted America
A Division of The History Press
Charleston, SC
www.historypress.net

Copyright © 2017 by Kathi Kresol
All rights reserved

First published 2017

Manufactured in the United States

ISBN 9781467137294

Library of Congress Control Number: 2017940924

To my own children: Sarah, Brandon, Amber, Aryn and Stacy. You make all things seem possible. And all the other children who are not mine but have touched my life through the years. Thank you for trusting me with your dreams and for inspiring me to reach for mine.

CONTENTS

CONTENTS

FOREWORD

When one brings up the subject of ghosts in the state of Illinois, Chicago is often touted as having more supernatural tales than any other city. Move over Chicago, Rockford has made a name for itself due in part to *Haunted Rockford, Illinois,* by author and historian Kathi Kresol. Many in northwest Illinois call her the Ghost Lady.

I first met Kresol around five years ago, and I was deeply impressed not only by her ability to constantly and completely book up every single ghost event, tour and lecture that she was part of but as a ghost researcher, colleague and friend. Her diligence and tireless efforts shine through everything she touches and has made her one of the most well-known and highly respected paranormal researchers and ghost event planners in the entire state.

I have been privileged to have worked with her numerous times over the past several years, and every time has been very special for me. I was awestruck at the vast amount of knowledge she has acquired over the years, especially when planning something for her immensely popular Haunted Rockford Tours events. I always listened intently as she laid out not only the haunted stories associated with a location but the incredibly detailed and researched history that has to be a part of every paranormal investigation. As I have always stated in the past, history and hauntings go hand in hand. One must first grasp the history of a locale as to what may have precipitated the hauntings to occur in the first place. Kresol leaves no stone unturned when addressing the background of a haunted site.

FOREWORD

As a librarian by trade, she spends a great deal of time delving into the past to get everything paranormally and historically correct. As a ghost researcher myself for the past forty-one years, I know from experience that the hardest and most tedious job has always been the historical research. The actual paranormal investigation and evidence gathering is by far the easier of the two. Kresol shines like a bright beacon of light in the dark cave of knowledge. Very few people that I have come across in my many contacts do it better. The information that she has amassed over the years would be fodder for a great many encyclopedias. As pop artist Carly Simon related in her popular James Bond song, "The Spy Who Loved Me," "Nobody does it better." And nobody does it better than Kresol.

I have waited with bated breath for the release of her long-overdue book *Haunted Rockford, Illinois.* While I researched the state for ghostly locations, Kresol chugged away, accumulating amazing stories in the Rockford area. These will be the subject of her second book and one that I cannot wait to read. Akin to a child's craving for candy, my craving has reached a fever pitch for the release of *Haunted Rockford, Illinois.*

Kresol has not simply compiled a few scary ghost tales in her book. What you will find are brilliantly researched and written cross-sections of a very haunted city, related in a fashion no one else can. Kresol is a "one of a kind" person who puts her nose to the grindstone and gets the job done in an unbelievable way.

If you buy only one book this year on ghosts, don't pass on this one because it's a gem! The streets, alleyways and cemeteries of Rockford are indeed haunted, and you will need a guide to take you there. This is truly your paranormal map to those many famous and infamous places that lurk in the shadows of Rockford.

Haunted Rockford, Illinois already has a place reserved for it in my supernatural library, and it should also be in yours.

DALE KACZMAREK
President of the Ghost Research Society
Director of Excursions into the Unknown Inc.

ACKNOWLEDGEMENTS

I wish to start by saying that I have been so completely overwhelmed by the support that I have received from those who read *Murder and Mayhem in Rockford, Illinois*! Thank you to all who bought, read, borrowed and shared my writings or took time to attend an event. I wish to thank Ben Gibson from The History Press, who showed tremendous patience during the process of collecting photographs for both books. The rest of the team was extremely helpful as well. They made the process so much easier than I expected it to be.

I owe a huge debt of gratitude to my co-workers at the Rockford Public Library. Besides being astounded every day with the amazing work you do for our community, I am humbled by the support you have given me through the years.

I have met many fascinating people involved in different aspects of history and the paranormal. Steve Litteral, the executive director of Tinker Swiss Cottage Museum who didn't hesitate to start down the paranormal path with me, is a wonderful historian and a fantastic storyteller. Steve and I partner to host the annual Illinois Paranormal Conference, and his incredible sense of humor makes him a joy to be around. Scott Lewandowski, the manager of the Veterans Memorial Hall and president of the Rockford Historical Society, has done so much for me. My partner in crime, Sara Bowker, psychic extraordinaire, has quirky humor and a sense of adventure that always amaze me. And the newest member of the Haunted Rockford team, Amanda Becker, is a fantastic historian and teacher. We connected over the story of a little murdered boy, Dickie Tebbets, whose death touched both of our lives.

Others who have assisted with the tours by opening their doors to my inquiry of "Got ghosts?" include Yolanda and Stanley Weisensel at Camp Grant Museum and Command Post Restaurant; Marty Mangas and Dee Hufstedler at the Coronado Performing Arts Center and their incredible crew of Land of Lincoln Theater Organ Society volunteers; Dr. Ray Kleinhaus, former event coordinator of the Briggs Mansion; Mike Grasso and his wife, Shari, of the Haunted Conover Square Ghost Tours; the staff at the Burpee Natural History Museum, who opened both of their historical homes; and Mark Tietz from Lucerne's Restaurant, who is a complete gem to work with. I owe a special thank-you to Kreena Robbins and her husband, Ian, who own the Hope and Anchor English Pub. Kreena helped me host the first Haunted Pub Bus Tour two years ago and continues to offer support. Mike Du Pre of Der Rathskeller and Zack Rotello from the Olympic Tavern were also great hosts for the tour. Sue Lewandowksi of the Ethnic Heritage Museum heads up a crew of wonderful volunteers who always make hosting a Haunted Rockford event at their location a joy.

I need to also thank fellow author Mike Kleen, who started me down this path by believing people would be interested in reading the stories I tell; Bill Gorman, who wrote *Ghost Whispers* and worked with me and Dave Oberg to host the first Haunted Rockford Tour through the Rockford Public Library; Stephen Osborne, another author and supporter who told me, "You can do this!" and whose sense of humor helped get me through the many hours of paranormal investigating; and Troy Taylor and Lisa Taylor-Horton, who always make me feel so welcomed at their events. I also want to thank Paul and Lisa Smith for their advice and assistance and all of the paranormal investigation teams that I have had the privilege of working with over the years: the now disbanded Forest City Paranormal, TnT Paranormal, Ghost Head Soup, Wisconsin-Illinois Paranormal Investigation Team (WIPIT), Society for Anomalous Studies, Paranormal Investigators of Milwaukee and the delightful Travis Dahlhauser and Chad Glovier from the Greater Rockford Apparition and Ghost Group (GRAGG). Laura Furman with the Midway Village Museum is an incredible source of information and an accommodating hostess for our events.

My appreciation also goes to the members of the Rockford Historical Society, who have offered me a seat at their table, advice for research and leads to great stories and whose enthusiasm and love for Rockford's history has been such an inspiration.

ACKNOWLEDGEMENTS

I especially owe a debt of gratitude to the ever-humble Dale Kaczmarek. Dale attends my events even when we are not co-hosting. His team members from the Ghost Research Society are very professional and patient and always ready no matter what happens. The support of someone as reputable, respected and experienced as Dale has helped more than he will ever know.

And as always, I would like to thank my family: my brother, Tom, web guy extraordinaire; my ever-supportive stepmother, Sharon Saunders, and my sister, Mari, amazing women who always inspire me; my mom and dad, Tom and Bette Saunders, for inspiring my love of history; and especially my children—Sarah, Brandon, Amber, Aryn and Stacy (and their partners)—for their never-wavering support and understanding when I am away running down stories or locked away writing and researching. You are the reason I always try just a little bit harder and push just a little further. Last but not least is John, who always knows exactly the right things to say and the right amount of chocolate to bring. I could not do this without you.

INTRODUCTION

I know some of you might be wondering about the title of this book, *Haunted Rockford, Illinois*. Are there really ghosts in Rockford? First, let me start with telling you that I am not writing this book to convince any of you that ghosts are real. That has never been my goal. My goal for telling these tales is to share the stories of the people who once called Rockford home.

Next, people will usually ask why I think Rockford is haunted. I do not claim to be an expert on anything, but I have spent a lot of time researching ghosts and hauntings. There are several theories why certain places might become haunted. Some people think certain items help conduct paranormal energy and that makes it easier for spirits to communicate with the living. One of these items is water, such as a river or a creek. Another condition is a Native American influence. Finally, limestone is also supposed to be a good conductor for spirits. Rockford has all three of these, especially in the downtown area.

According to Charles A. Church in his book *A History of Rockford and Winnebago County, Illinois* (New English Society, 1900), two-thirds of Winnebago County is underlined by Galena limestone. Church also explains that the Rock River is lined with hundreds of mounds left behind by the ancient tribes, predecessors to the Native Americans who were here long before the white man came. These mounds were mostly ceremonial like the ones left in Beattie Park. They were estimated to number in the hundreds, and some say there were as many as five hundred within Winnebago County. Some of the mounds were found to contain burials

Illinois Boat and Dock, Rockford, Ill.

The Illinois boat and dock is located behind the present-day Rockford Public Library. *From Midway Village Museum, Rockford, Illinois.*

of these native people. Unfortunately, farmers and builders plowed them under, only rarely contacting archaeologists for assistance. The scientists would conduct their digs and recover the bodies and burial objects to take back with them. One account spoke of a skeleton found in Beattie Park when early settlers were breaking the ground to build homes. The skeleton belonged to a little child about five years old. The care taken with the burial and the objects placed in the grave revealed the level of feeling attached to the death of this child. The story told of the sadness experienced by everyone who witnessed the uncovering of the small bones. Along with the sadness, there was also awe that came from the realization that those little bones belonged to a child who had played in that exact location well over 1,500 years ago.

That leads to another theory for paranormal activity. Intense emotion, whether good or bad, can leave an imprint on the environment. The very landscape of a location carries the footprint of all the different people who have come before. Anyone who has ever visited historic places will understand this theory. Places of great tragedies, such as battlefields or concentration camps, can prove this point all too clearly. There are those places where the veil that separates the present and the past feels very thin. It is possible, one supposes, to pull back the veil for just a moment and glimpse into the past.

These things all combine together to conduct the paranormal activity and make it easier for the spirits to communicate. Now, as I stated before, I am no expert in the paranormal field. I have researched the local stories here for a decade. But let me quickly point out that I have dealt with living people for a whole lot longer, and I can't figure them out either!

Rockford has a wonderful tapestry of history that is woven together with all the stories of the different people who have called it home. It is always these stories that motivate me to keep following those breadcrumbs. So I will let you decide for yourself if these are just interesting legends that have been passed down or they are true ghostly encounters. For maybe it is like Albert Einstein once said, "The most beautiful thing we can experience is the mysterious."

From author's collection.

Part I

GHOSTLY ENCOUNTERS

The boundaries which divide Life from Death are at best shadowy and vague.
Who shall say where the one ends, and where the other begins?
—Edgar Allan Poe

1

THE TERRIBLE TRAGEDY OF GERALDINE BOURBON

M y family bought the old farmhouse on School Street in 1988 knowing nothing about the violent incident that had occurred there. This was our first house, and it seemed like our dream home. It was big enough for our four children, had a big yard and was three blocks away from my husband's elderly father.

The sale and the move went so smoothly, it seemed as though it was meant to be. Almost immediately strange things started happening. We would put items down, and they would show up in a totally different area. It was easy to convince ourselves it was the kids moving the items. We had four children under the age of five, and our lives were very busy.

There were certain times it was too much to ignore. The paper towel rack in the kitchen had a habit of emptying by itself. It was always when I placed a new roll on the rack. It would unroll until all the paper was on the floor. The lights would also flicker, and the television would turn on all by itself. This usually happened after everyone was upstairs in bed. We would suddenly be awakened by the noises from the television down on the first floor.

Every once in a while, we would get the feeling of being watched. We knew from the woman we purchased the house from that a family member had died in the house from natural causes. The house was built in 1913, and many families had lived there; we always reasoned that the identity of our ghost was one of the former family members.

We had several pets over the years, and at times, they would behave strangely. They would always seem to watch something over our heads. The cats would hunker down and emit a low growling sound. It was disconcerting to see them react to something we could not see. One of our small dogs seemed especially affected. We had one particular friend, Nathan, whom this dog did not like. Nathan was a teenager who helped us with yard work and whom I tutored while my children were in school. The dog would growl at Nathan and bite his shoes. Once we were sitting in the dining room, and Nathan was getting frustrated because the dog would not leave him alone. The dog kept going under the table and biting his shoes, and Nathan would shake him off and tell him to stop. The dog finally backed off and left the room.

A few minutes went by, and we heard this horrible howling noise. It was coming from the upstairs of the house. There were four bedrooms on the second floor, and the master bedroom had a hook and eye up toward the top of the door to keep the children away from the guns that my husband stored in the closet.

Nathan and I followed the howling and realized it was coming from that room. We unlocked the door, and the dog came rushing out and ran down the stairs. We never solved the mystery of how the dog got locked into that room. Nathan was so shaken by the incident that he left immediately.

I was constantly remodeling the old farmhouse and had problems with the electrical tools. I would be taking a break in another room, and the tools would turn on by themselves. It was frustrating because it would never happen when I was in the room, only when I stepped away for a minute. One time when I was working with a palm sander, I left for a moment, and the tool turned on. By this time, I was getting agitated, so I unplugged it from the wall. I went back into the kitchen, and as soon as I rounded the corner, I heard the sander turn on again. I threw the sander away.

The turning point was an incident with a baby bottle. I ran a daycare in the home, so my youngest child had her name on her bottles to keep them separate from the other children's. I spell her name Aryn (pronounced Erin). One night, I put Aryn in her crib in the room where the two youngest children slept. I gave her a bottle and went back downstairs to finish cleaning up from dinner. A little while later, she started to cry. I went to check on her and noticed the bottle was gone. I looked all over the room for the bottle. I didn't find it, so I went back down the stairs and made her a fresh one. I remember thinking it was odd the way it just disappeared seemingly into thin air.

Life went on, and the children got older. We were still remodeling the house and began the process on the second floor in the room that was the youngest girl's bedroom. It had old wiring, and the plaster had some holes. So we decided to tear the room out completely. I was breaking down the plaster and tearing out the lathe boards. The process was going smoothly but messily

The house on School Street. *From* Rockford Morning Star.

when I came across something odd. Behind the plaster and the lathe boards inside the wall was a pink baby bottle. The baby bottle had Aryn's name on it.

After that I couldn't ignore what was happening any longer. I started to research the house. I knew some of the neighbors on the block had lived in their houses for many years. I interviewed them and they told me that someone had been killed in our house. They thought it happened in the summer of 1958. I went to the Rockford Public Library and started to go through the microfilm files for the summer of 1958. I found nothing. I wasn't sure quite what to do, so I decided to start in the beginning of the year, just in case.

I'll never forget the feeling that swept over me when I came to the article telling of Geraldine Bourbon's murder on January 18, 1958. There, on the front page of the newspaper, was my house. The story told of the horrible deaths of Geraldine and Laurence. I felt the hairs rise on the back of my neck.

Geraldine was just an average woman who lived in Rockford during the 1950s. I first came across her name in that newspaper article when I was researching our house on School Street. I immediately noticed a few similarities. We had both lived in the same house, and we were both mothers of small children. We both had family members who were in the armed services; Geraldine was married to an army officer, and my father was in the navy. Both of us had moved around because of this. We both had struggled with issues in our marriages.

There were some differences between us, though. I would leave the house on the West Side of Rockford, and I would live to see twenty-nine years old. Geraldine would do neither.

Geraldine's childhood was easy to trace. She was one of four daughters born to Maxine and Percy Tonnancour. Geraldine was born in Wisconsin in 1929. Their family was close knit, and the other children stayed in proximity to their parents but not Geraldine; she was not content to live in the same small town all her life.

Geraldine married twice. She was very young when she married the first time. They had two children and were not married very long when they divorced. Geraldine's two children stayed with their father in Wisconsin.

Laurence Ray Bourbon's life was not as easy to trace as Geraldine's. He was the only boy in the family; he and his sister, Florence Fay, were twins. For some reason, the family went to St. Louis in 1929, but Florence and Laurence were boarded with another family across the state back in their hometown. There was no reason given for this or information on how long the family was separated.

Laurence and Geraldine met and were married in 1951, when Geraldine was twenty-one. He was in the army, and though he was not traditionally what you would call handsome, his uniform made him attractive. Geraldine must have thought that traveling with her husband would bring the adventure she sought.

By September 1957, the couple had two children and were living in Germany. Laurence was suffering from mental health issues and had a drinking problem. These issues eventually led to his undesirable discharge from the army. The family left Germany and moved to Rockford, where some of Geraldine's family lived. The couple moved into a little apartment on Grant Street and then moved again to Court Street. Laurence started a job in construction, and Geraldine stayed at home with the children. The couple struggled, and these challenges led to issues in the marriage.

Geraldine was close to her sister Arline, and she shared her concerns about her marriage. Geraldine stated that Laurence was violent, and she had become very frightened of him. On January 9, 1958, there was an altercation, and Geraldine was terrified enough to finally leave Laurence. She took the children, filed for divorce and moved in with Arline and her husband, William. Geraldine told the court that Laurence had become increasingly violent, and in his latest attack, he struck not only her but also their four-year-old daughter, Kathleen.

Laurence was apologetic and tried several times to reconcile, but Geraldine remained at her sister and brother-in-law's house on School Street. On January 17, 1958, Laurence tried once again to reconcile by calling Geraldine and begging her to take him back. She again refused.

The two sisters were sitting in the kitchen of the School Street house around eleven o'clock that Friday morning. One of Arline's young sons wanted to go outside to play for a while. Arline bundled him up, and he left the house through the back door. Neither of the women noticed that the boy didn't lock the door as he left.

A few moments later, the peace of the morning was shattered. The door flew open, and Laurence stood there in the doorway, shouting that he was going to "kill her" and waving a gun. Geraldine ran around the corner into the living room. Arline saw her chance to get help and ran next door to the auto body shop.

Thomas Guzzo was the owner of the shop and he stepped out of his office as Arline came inside screaming for help. Guzzo listened to her story and then headed for the phone to call the police.

Arline realized the children were all still in the house and bravely headed back next door to get them to safety. As she left the garage, she looked up to the second-story window to see her sister waving frantically and pounding on the bedroom window. One of Arline's sons was upstairs during the altercation, and she was frantic for his safety. As she hurried to get the other children out of the house, she screamed to him to get to the bathroom and lock the door.

The evidence would show that Laurence initially attacked Geraldine in the living room. Arline's children had scattered and the only witness left was Kathleen, Geraldine's four-year-old daughter. Little Kathleen told police that Laurence was shouting and hitting her mother. Laurence then shot Geraldine in the back of her head. Geraldine ran up the stairs to the bedroom, trying to get away from him.

Unfortunately, there was no escape. Laurence caught up with Geraldine in the bedroom and shot her a second time. Her wounds proved too much for her, and she fell dead. Laurence caught her and placed her gently on the bed.

The police arrived in record time and saw Laurence hanging halfway out of the front upstairs window. They headed to the back of the house after first trying the front door. A shot rang out just as they burst through the door.

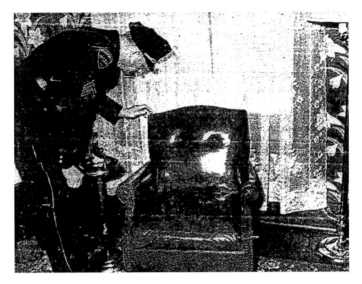

A bloodied chair. *From* Rockford Register Republic.

The Bourbon children and their grandmother Maxine. *From* Rockford Morning Star.

The murder weapon. *From Rockford Register Republic.*

Laurence had stretched out on the bed next to his wife and put the pistol under his chin. When he pulled the trigger he sealed their fates forever.

Laurence "loved" Geraldine too much to let her leave him, and the energy created by his last selfish act continues to resonate through the whole house. I visited the house recently with a psychic. The psychic agreed that Laurence and Geraldine are still there. You can feel the tension all around the house. It breaks my heart to think of Geraldine still trapped there, reliving her last terrifying moments. The thought of Laurence there waiting to feed on someone's anger and fear is terrifying.

We had been in that house for ten years by then, and I knew that as long as we stayed there, we would always be a part of that struggle between Geraldine and Laurence. I also wondered how that struggle between them affected my family. This all took place before the paranormal got so popular. There were no investigation teams in Rockford then. There was no one to offer advice to homeowners on what to do when you suspected that your house might have a ghost. I decided to move. It was the best decision I ever made.

Geraldine's story touched me and changed my life. I started to research other local stories about the paranormal. I feel almost compelled to share these of other places and families that had similar experiences.

2

BARNES MANSION

ECHOES FROM THE PAST

There is a beautiful home that has stood on the west side of the Rock River since 1893. It was built by William Fletcher Barnes for his family. The Barnes family sold the house to the Rockford Park District in 1937, and it was used for the park's offices for several years before the second and third floors became the Burpee Museum of Natural History in 1942. Today, the beautiful building is once again used as administration offices for the museum.

The museum was thrilled when it acquired the building, but it had no idea what else it got in the bargain. According to the staff, some of the former inhabitants of the building are still occupying the home they loved.

The house is located right on the banks of the Rock River. It is also down the street from Beattie Park, which has several Native American effigy mounds. According to the website Genealogy Trails, there were hundreds of mounds located up and down the Rock. Both of these conditions, along with the limestone that sits under most of downtown Rockford, make the Barnes Mansion a prime spot for paranormal activity.

Another theory that the Barnes home fits is the idea that people can leave imprints on certain locations, especially in times of heightened emotions, good or bad. This is evident when you visit historical places that seem able to almost transport you back into the past. These places, like the Barnes Mansion, have layers of history, some ancient, as in the case of the Native Americans, but some more recent.

The Barnes Mansion. *From author's collection.*

The Barnes family suffered many tragedies while they lived in the house, and these, according to some paranormal theories, also help make a place more apt to become haunted.

The staff at Burpee has had several unexplainable incidents inside the building. The sounds of long-forgotten music have been heard in the halls of the home. A former employee whose office was on the first floor of the three-story building shared an incident she experienced in the house during an interview. She stated that she was in her office on the first floor late one evening when she heard music that seemed to be coming from a different floor. The second floor of the building also contains offices, and the employee assumed one of her co-workers must still be in the building, listening to a radio. She finished her work and decided to check to see if her co-worker was ready to depart so they might leave together.

The music was definitely coming from a room on the second floor, and though there was no light on in the office, the employee decided to check the room anyway. She lifted her foot to step into the room, and the music suddenly stopped. As she stood there in the darkened doorway she felt a cold draft blow by her, chilling her. She turned to look back down the hallway and felt as though someone had stepped behind her. She decided that it was time to leave and rushed back down to her office to collect her things. Later, she described the music as not from this time period.

William Barnes's family moved to Rockford in the 1850s. William, along with several brothers, created a business to manufacture woodworking machines. They were very successful and sold their products not only in Rockford but worldwide. The business proved to be so lucrative that even during the Panic of 1893, it continued to expand when many others were forced to close down.

When time came to build his growing family a home, William decided to build a showplace that he and his wife, Julia, could be proud to call their own. Since their business was building woodworking machines, he decided to fill it with beautiful woodwork. William was a good businessman, and he hired many of the recently unemployed carpenters to complete the unique woodwork pieces he planned for his home. The large house has fifteen rooms, a turret and hand-carved cherry paneling in the foyer, reception area and first-floor hallway. The house was considered one of the finest houses in Rockford, and many thought that the Barnes family seemed to lead golden lives; unfortunately, that all would change.

William and his wife, Julia, had four children during their marriage: two daughters, Katherine and Aimee, who were said to be as beautiful as their mother, and two sons, Joseph and William Fletcher Jr. (called W.F. by his family). Joseph took after his father and would follow in his footsteps. W.F. took a different route in life and became passionate about automobiles when they arrived on the scene. He ordered one of the first cars ever delivered to Rockford. W.F. went against William's wishes and faced being disinherited when he decided to become a race car driver. William eventually forgave his son and helped him finance one of the first car dealerships in Rockford.

William and Julia loved all of their children, but William had a special bond with his son Joseph. Joseph left Rockford after high school to continue his education in engineering at Cornell College in Iowa. After his education, Joseph returned to Rockford to work next to his father and uncles in the drafting department of the business. He was such a hardworking young man that he quickly rose to vice-president of the company. Joseph was respected by all who knew him.

In 1902, Joseph married Adeline Stewart, and the couple later had two children. By all accounts, the future could not have been brighter for the Barnes family. All that would quickly end, however. In 1905, tragedy struck the family when Joseph died unexpectedly from typhoid. Joseph's funeral was held in the home on North Main Street.

It is this tragedy that started a downward spiral for the family. It is also this event that might have caused some of the paranormal incidents later reported by staff. It was customary at the time of Joseph's death for the funeral to be held in the family home. Joseph's body was placed in a room in the basement in preparation for the service.

The basement area of the house is the focus of many claims of paranormal incidents. Staff and visitors have experienced the feeling of being watched all throughout this floor. They have also reported being overwhelmed by a sense of anxiety or sadness.

By all accounts, Joseph's death devastated the entire Barnes family. William was especially affected by the death and seemed to lose interest in the business. He soon sold his portion of the family business to H.L. Pratt.

Psychics Paul Smith and Sara Bowker also state that there may be another reason why the Barnes house carries such a bad vibration in this area. During the early days of the Burpee Museum, one of the more unusual displays on exhibit was a complete skeleton of a Native American that was supposed to be from this region. Paul and Sara claim that this would definitely leave an imprint in the house. The practice of displaying the bodies of Native Americans is no longer conducted by the museum.

The family suffered another unbelievable blow when their grandson who was named after their son Joseph was killed in 1910. The seven-year-old was staying with his maternal grandparents while his mother was on her honeymoon. Mrs. Adeline Stewart Barnes married her second husband, Archie Catlin of Kansas, in her parents' home less than twenty-four hours before the horrible accident.

Joseph and his cousin were downtown with Adeline's sister and were apparently told to wait for her in the car. Joseph was described as a lively little boy who was easily bored. He decided to crawl out of the car, not realizing the danger. Witnesses stated later that they saw Joseph leave the car and were horrified to see another car bearing down on him. Several people yelled, but there was nothing they could do but watch helplessly as the boy darted out in the street and the vehicle ran him down. It was determined that the driver could not have avoided the little boy. Joseph was laid to rest next to his father at Greenwood Cemetery.

Another tragedy occurred when William's lovely wife, Julia, was part of a camping trip to Manitowish, Wisconsin. Julia was walking in the woods and was injured when a hunter accidently shot her. She took most of the charge to the side of her face. One of the shots passed through her eye. Julia was carried to camp by her son W.F. Barnes Jr., who then accompanied her to

Mrs. Julia Barnes. *From* Rockford Morning Star.

Chicago. Julia would not tell authorities who shot her, stating only that it was an accident. Julia would recover from her wounds, but she suffered from chronic pain for the rest of her life. She was no longer able to attend the lavish parties that she once hosted. Julia passed away in 1922, but according to psychics, she still stands looking out the second-floor windows of her beautiful home.

In 1928, William became ill and was bedridden before he died from a stroke on December 30, 1930. He was survived by his son W.F. Barnes and his daughter Amy Barnes Lane. Amy would decide to sell the house to the Rockford Park District in 1937.

Haunted Rockford was hosting a tour through the building and paranormal investigator Dale Kaczmarek attended. He was using a device called an Ovilus. In simplified terms, an Ovilus is a machine used by ghost hunters that allegedly modulates changes in the environment and converts them into speech. This allows the spirits to communicate directly with the investigator. Shortly after turning on the device in the basement, the words "it hurts, you asshole" came through quite clearly.

Other staff members tell of the times when they have closed up the building and shut off all the lights before setting the alarm. They walk out to the parking lot only to realize that all of the lights have been turned on again, though no one was left in the building. At first, the staff would go back in and shut off the lights, but they would be back on by the time they reached their cars. Now they simply leave them on.

Haunted Rockford also hosted a paranormal investigation for the public in the mansion. While the investigation team was on a preliminary tour to decide where equipment should be placed, several of the female members felt as if someone was touching their hair. The team leader, also a woman, heard someone sigh in her ear. She felt as well as heard this. There is a large closet on the second floor, and people have claimed to feel fear and anxiety by the door. According to psychics, this feeling is caused by a man that was once employed by the Barnes family. Apparently, this man would wait for the young maids or nannies to go to the room to put something away, and then he would step in behind them, trapping them in the room. He would grope and fondle them against their will, causing them to become very upset. He would threaten them by telling them he would get them fired if they told. "This was a bad man," psychic Sara Bowker emphasized.

There have also been reports of shadows moving around on the second and third floors of the house. These have been seen by staff as well as visitors. There is another room on the third floor that seems to be disturbing to certain people. It is a strange little room that has a sink and might have been used as a staff lounge or a workroom during the museum days. Several people that entered that room on the night of the investigation felt a sense of vertigo by stepping across the threshold. They complained of being dizzy, short of breath and very anxious.

Whether it is a combination of certain conditions or the rich history of the house, the Barnes Mansion is clearly a unique place where the lines that separate the present and the past become blurry. The beautiful building still showcases the wonderful skill of the builders who constructed it. And the love of the owners for their home shines through the entire house as much today as it did when the Barneses proudly entertained there. Though no children play here anymore and some of the rooms are vacant of any furnishings, the Barnes Mansion still echoes with the sounds of the family members who continue to roam these halls.

3

MANNY MANSION

THE SMALLEST OF GHOSTS

The distinctive limestone house that sits on the west bank of the Rock River is best known today for being a part of the Burpee Museum of Natural History. The museum is a gem itself and is a must-see for visitors and locals alike. While many visitors may come to see the dinosaurs and other remnants of creatures that lived here long ago, few may realize that the home attached to the museum is quite haunted.

As mentioned in the chapter about the Barnes Mansion, certain items seem to make good conductors for paranormal activity, and the Manny Mansion contains some of these. The Native American influence, the location on the Rock River and the house's construction using limestone all combine to increase the probability of paranormal activity.

The house was built in 1852 by John Coleman, who moved his family here from New York. John married Cornelia Townsend in 1833, and they had four children by the time they arrived in Rockford. John was a successful businessman and became the president of the Rockford Water Company. Later his family became involved in banking and John was a partner in Robertson, Coleman and Company. He also served as a trustee for Rockford Seminary and a member of the city council.

The family continued to live in the house all the way through 1864, when John Coleman became ill and the decision was made to sell the house to John Pels Manny. John Pels Manny's family also came from New York. They settled in Waddam's Grove, Illinois, around 1842, and it was there that John met and married Eunice Hicks in 1848.

The Manny Mansion. *From Midway Village Museum, Rockford.*

By 1852, John had begun to work with his cousin John H. Manny to design reapers for wheat, and the decision was made to move to Rockford. John's family had begun to grow, and though the number of children born to the family by 1864 is unclear, the fact that most of them passed away quite young stands out.

The family moved into the lovely home and improved the property. By 1867, Eunice had given birth to at least five children and lost all but the eldest boy, George, who turned seventeen in 1867. When their youngest daughter, Katie, was two, she contracted tuberculosis and died on February 16, 1867. It was said that Eunice's heart broke with the death

John Pels Manny. *From the Rockford Public Library.*

35

The Manny monument is located at Greenwood Cemetery. *From author's collection.*

of yet another baby. Eunice herself passed away a little over a month later, on March 23, 1867. John built a beautiful monument at Greenwood Cemetery to honor his family. It was sculpted in Rome by Leonard Volk and is still one of the most impressive monuments in the cemetery.

John P. continued to invent many different farm machines, and his contribution to the Manny reaper blades was monumental. He opened the John P. Manny Company with partners Elias Cosper and Melancthon Starr. John Pels eventually remarried in 1868. His second wife, Florida Lucretia, was a daughter of his partner Melancthon.

The couple lived in the limestone house and had five children there. One of their little ones, Lucretia, also died young, only reaching one year old before she passed away in 1872. John P.'s reaper business ran into financial issues in the 1880s, and the family sold the house to the Nelson family (of the Nelson Knitting Company fame) in 1889.

John Pels died in 1897. He was elected president of the West Side Cemetery Association, which later become Greenwood Cemetery, in 1876 and served on the board until his death. His death was sudden and caused by typhoid, which came from drinking contaminated water at the cemetery one day while he was working there. His death struck the Rockford community hard, and the newspapers were filled with tributes from his fellow businessmen.

The history of the Nelson family is also very impressive, but the ghostly encounters in the home seem to originate from the period it was occupied by the Manny family.

In 1935, Harry Burpee was a furniture maker and an undertaker. He decided to purchase the property with the intention of opening a funeral home at the location. Several of the neighbors objected to this idea, so Harry decided to locate the funeral home on Church Street instead.

Harry and his wife, Della, never lived in the Manny Mansion but decided to turn it into the Harry and Della Burpee Art Gallery. They built an auditorium and the gallery addition in 1939. The decision was made in 1986 to move the art to the present Riverfront Museum Park location. The Rockford Art Museum is there still along with the Discovery Center and the Rockford Dance Company. The Manny Mansion was then renovated to locate the Burpee Museum of Natural History offices, classrooms and the Native American exhibit.

Several paranormal investigation teams have assisted with the investigations hosted by Haunted Rockford over the years. They all have used different techniques, with varied results, to inspire the ghosts to connect during these sessions. All of the teams agree that something paranormal is definitely going on in the house and suggest further investigations.

Some of the staff claims are very similar to the experiences at the Barnes Mansion next door. There has been old-time music heard, doors that open and close and lights that seem to go off and on without any reason. The main difference is that in the Manny Mansion, most of the claims seem to be small shadows that dart from room to room, especially on the second floor.

The Manny Mansion was at that time one of the grandest homes in Rockford. The house was always very beautiful, and during the time the Manny and Nelson families occupied it, the house became the center of Rockford's social scene. There were lavish parties thrown, and the newspapers would go into great detail about the orchestras on the lawn, the carriages lining the lantern-lit driveway and the impressive guest lists. There were also beautiful weddings and several funerals conducted in the home through the years.

The outside of the house is still lovely, but the inside has been made into classrooms and offices for the Burpee Museum of Natural History. The once grand home's interior has been changed to meet the current needs of the organization, and apparently, John Pels Manny and his two wives are not very pleased by this decision. Some of the EVPs (electronic voice phenomena) picked up seem to point toward the fact that the families who once occupied the location are not happy about the changes that have been made to their home.

Psychics Paul Smith and Sara Bowker have worked with Haunted Rockford during these events and shared the former homeowners' displeasure. They have also mentioned that the two Mrs. Mannys each claim to be the true mistress of the house. The two wives are aware of each other but never communicate.

But it is the children who are the strongest presences in the home. According to Smith and Bowker, the children run up and down the stairs, and their shadows are the ones that have been seen going from room to room. They stay in the home because it was here that they were the happiest. They like to play tricks on the staff by turning on and off lights and shutting or opening doors.

During one of the investigations, the name Nelly was picked up on an EVP. On another session, Paul Smith also picked up the name and said that Nelly once was a nanny to the children in the home. This claim was validated by researching the census records. The family had an eighteen-year-old servant girl named Nelly living with them in 1880. According to Smith, she continues to care for the children.

John Pels and both of his wives, Eunice and Florida, loved their distinctive home on North Main Street and were very proud of it and their contributions to the Rockford community. Though the home is changed on the inside, you can imagine that they are still proud of the fact that the Burpee Museum of Natural History continues their legacy of serving families in Rockford and the surrounding area.

4

CAMP GRANT

TRAGEDY AND TRIUMPH

The Camp Grant Museum and Command Post Restaurant is a treasure-trove of interesting history told through actual artifacts of the men and women who served at Camp Grant. It is owned by Stanley and Yolanda Weisensel. They have spent many years scouring the area on a quest to build a memorial to the people who traveled through this area on their way to serve our country in World Wars I and II.

The place is fascinating enough on its own, but the Weisensels are gems themselves. Yolanda is quite a storyteller and has spent many hours researching the whole area that once was Camp Grant.

The construction for Camp Grant began in July 1917, and by November of that year, 1,100 buildings had been constructed. It was designed to be a training site for infantry, engineers, machine gunners and artillery. Both enlisted men and officers were trained there.

It was virtually a small city and even had its own fire department and police force. It also included a base hospital, a photography studio, a movie theater and a parade ground. It totaled over five thousand acres. In its peak time, July 1918, Camp Grant supported a total of 50,543 officers and enlisted men.

The fall of 1918 brought a new commandant to Camp Grant. Colonel Charles B. Hagadorn had an almost spotless career in the armed services. He graduated from West Point on June 14, 1889, and returned as a drawing instructor. Hagadorn also served in Manilla. It was here that, according to the newspapers, Charles experienced bitter fighting.

The only spot on his respectable career was when Hagadorn was assigned to the position as a military attaché in Petrograd, Russia. Charles

The inside of the Camp Grant Museum and Command Post Restaurant. *From author's collection.*

This postcard provides a bird's-eye view of Camp Grant. *From Midway Village Museum, Rockford.*

President Roosevelt visits Camp Grant. *From Midway Village Museum, Rockford.*

requested a transfer from the position in 1914 citing health issues. The government denied his request, and Charles left anyway, stating later that he needed medical care that was not available in Manilla.

Charles Hagadorn was mildly disciplined after his return and soon the incident was forgotten. Hagadorn became the commandant of Camp Grant in September 1918.

Shortly after the new commandant arrived in the fall of 1918, the devastating Spanish flu hit the Rockford area. This was a worldwide epidemic that killed millions. Hundreds of thousands of people died in the United States, and Rockford was hit very hard. The supposed cause of the massive spreading of this disease was the soldiers themselves. Looking back, it is no surprise that Camp Grant, with so many men in such close quarters, was devastated by the aggressive onslaught of the influenza. The first case was reported on September 23, 1918. Three days later, there were over seven hundred cases reported, and by the end of the month, over four thousand cases were reported.

Not much could be done to help the patients who came down with this dreaded disease. It swept quickly through the camp, and there were some twenty-four-hour periods when over one hundred men died. Within nine days, one thousand men had perished, and within two weeks, the number had swelled to over two thousand dead.

By early October, Colonel Hagadorn was showing signs of the stress from the massive loss of his men. He had suffered from insomnia for years,

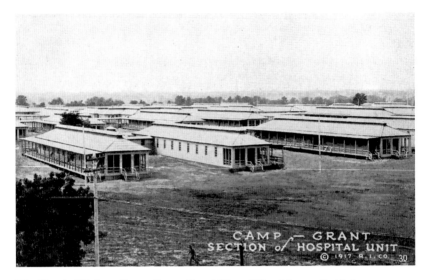

The Hospital Units at Camp Grant. *From Midway Village Museum, Rockford.*

but at this time, it became severe. Other officers who shared a house with him stated later that they heard him pacing and talking to himself at all hours of the night. On October 7, 1918, Hagadorn was heard to say, "My God, but these deaths are appalling!"

The next morning, Colonel Hagadorn was found dead in his bed. Though all of the soldiers were told that it was nervous exhaustion from the strain of all of the deaths at the camp, the newspapers from all over the country stated the truth. Charles Hagadorn had shot himself in the head. There were some people who speculated, however, that maybe it was not suicide at all. This was explored in a fictional book written by Carl Brown titled *No Taps for Charlie*. Brown apparently thought that Colonel Hagadorn was murdered, though this theory has never been proven. Within days of Colonel Hagadorn's death, the influenza outbreak began to slow, and by the end of October, it was considered to be controlled at the camp.

According to psychics Sara Bowker and Paul Smith, Colonel Hagadorn is one of the remaining spirits at the camp. His presence is very strong in every part of the building, and therefore, it is not surprising that he has been seen and heard by visitors. Both Sara and Paul think that he is still there trying to protect what he considers to be "his boys." They also state that he has a fondness for Yolanda and Stanley. They have told the soldiers' stories and ensured that these men would not be forgotten.

After the war, the camp was used for a variety of purposes, including a temporary training facility for the Illinois National Guard. The camp was

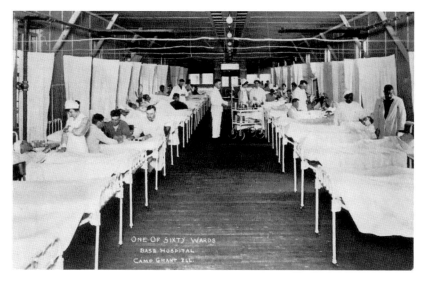

The inside of a hospital unit. *From Midway Village Museum, Rockford.*

reopened for World War II and in August 1943 began to house German POWs, most of whom were members of the German Afrika Corps or U-boat sailors. These men were paid to work in the nearby fields and canneries to help ease the shortage of men in the local area. Later, many of these prisoners would claim that they were treated very well at the camp. Some of them were drawn back to this area to live after the war.

Besides being filled with interesting artifacts, the museum also has many spirits that linger within its walls. The owners and waitstaff have had many experiences that they cannot explain. They have had items moved around, seen moving balls of light, felt someone touch them and seen full-bodied apparitions.

Right from the beginning, Yolanda knew there was something different about this place. She would set the tables up for the day shift each night before leaving. Upon their return in the morning, the place settings would be moved around. Sometimes it would be all the salt shakers, and the next it might be all the silverware; there was no rhyme or reason to it. It just seemed like something or someone was trying to get her attention.

One waitress was standing at the wait station before opening one morning and noticed some movement out of the corner of her eye. She froze and slowly turned her head. She could see a soldier standing an estimated six feet away from her. He was in uniform and he appeared solid. As she turned her head farther, to look at him fully, he disappeared.

There was another occasion when Yolanda's daughter, Toni, was at the restaurant after hours with a gentleman who was working on the computer. He needed to take a break to use the restroom, which was in the main part of the dining area. He was returning to the office area when he saw a rather large man with an apron step through a doorway from one of the exhibits rooms. The man, who was very solid, looked toward the computer man and scowled, as though he was not happy to see him.

The computer man returned to the office and asked Toni about who else might be in the building at that time of night. When Toni assured him that they were alone in the building, he shared what he saw with her. They left the building shortly after that.

Yolanda has had other experiences in the diner. Once, she was finishing up for the night and was leaning over her office chair typing on the computer when she felt a nudge on her shoulder. She assumed it was Stanley letting her know he was ready to go. When she turned to speak to him, there was no one there. She went into the dining room and found Stanley sitting at one of the tables. When she asked him if he was just in the office, he stated that he had been at the table the whole time.

Even with her earlier experiences, Yolanda was not convinced that the place might be haunted, but that all changed one evening. She was standing in the dining area talking to someone when she turned to look down the hallway past the bathrooms. Yolanda was astonished to see a young man dressed in a white apron run across the hallway from the Rockford room. He was laughing and turned to look back over his shoulder as if someone were chasing him. "He seemed to be having a good time," Yolanda stated later.

The staff hear new stories on almost a daily basis from families whose loved ones served at the camp or were held there as POWs during World War II. Yolanda receives letters, photographs and other artifacts. Once she even received a placemat from the first Thanksgiving dinner served there.

Yolanda and Stanley have worked very hard to ensure that this little piece of Rockford's history is not forgotten through the stories they share and the mementos and photographs they have collected. Psychics who have visited the place all feel that this has not gone unnoticed by the spirits that linger in this place. It seems to work almost as a "ghost magnet," and they appear drawn to the place. Perhaps they are waiting to have their stories told. All the psychics agree that the spirits are grateful to Yolanda and Stanley for honoring their memories.

Yolanda is very comfortable with the idea of the spirits staying around, as long as they stay at the restaurant. "I always say goodnight when I leave. I also tell them they can't come home with me. You stay here,." says Yolanda.

5

LITTLE GIRL LOST

There is a warehouse on the southeast side of Rockford that has an unusual problem. The problem isn't with wiring or plumbing; this warehouse has a ghost. Actually, it has a couple of them. But the most disturbing one is the ghost of a little girl. No one can remember when they started hearing stories about this little girl, but all agree it has been years.

The little girl is seen all over the area but mainly near the intersection of Samuelson Road and Sixth Street. Yolanda Weisensel, owner of Command Post Restaurant and Camp Grant Museum, states that she has heard quite a bit about the child. The little girl is described as being between five to eight years old, with long, light brown hair, and she wears a dress with stockings and boots. "She seems to be from the 1910s–1920s era. I have heard several stories. Someone told me they can remember a little girl who got hit by a train back when the train tracks ran down Sixth Street," Weisensel states.

There is one person who is reluctant to talk about the little girl, however. He works in the previously mentioned warehouse, and we will call him "Sam." "I was moving some pipes in the warehouse. I would bend over and pick up a pipe and move it to its new location," explained Sam. There is a door that has a window set in the top half, right across from where Sam was working, and what he saw in the reflection of the window startled him so much that he no longer likes to be in the warehouse at night by himself.

When Sam stood up with a pipe, he caught his reflection in the glass of the door. He had seen that same window at least a dozen times, but this

Top: A warehouse. *From author's collection.*

Bottom: Railroad tracks. *From author's collection.*

time, something was different. When Sam looked into the glass, he saw more than his own reflection. Standing next to him was the reflection of a little girl. She was about six or seven years old, had light brown hair and was wearing a dress. Even more alarming to Sam, the girl reached out for his hand, and just as he saw the little girl's hand touch his, his whole right arm went cold. Sam quickly looked next to him. There was no one there.

Sam turned to look back into the window, and the little girl was still there. Sam is not a man to frighten easily. He's a large man, six feet, three inches or so, and probably 230 pounds. But he shared with me that he is Samoan, and his Pacific Island people are very superstitious about the dead. The Pacific people believe that objects that reflect one's image are a portal to the spirit realm. To steal the souls of the living, evil spirits sometimes take on the appearance of loved ones who have passed away.

While others might have been curious and even possibly thrilled that the little girl had contacted them, Sam was not. He does not want to be disrespectful toward the little girl, but he really doesn't ever want to see her again.

Other people have seen this same little girl outside the building, skipping along both Sixth Street and Samuelson Roads and picking the wildflowers that grow up along the roadside. They claim that she is just as solid as any other living little girl. The only thing odd about her is she is dressed in clothes from another time. Despite research into the train accidents in that particular area and reviewing news reports on a child who died at that intersection, I have been unable to find the little girl's identity; she remains as elusive as her reason for lingering here.

6

CORONADO THEATER

WHERE THE SHOW GOES ON

The Coronado Performing Arts Center has been described as a jewel in the crown of all things that make Rockford great. It was the dream child of Willard and Erma Van Matre to create this beautiful theater. Willard Van Matre was born in Chicago on August 19, 1889. His family moved to Rockford when Willard was fourteen years old, sometime around 1903. The senior Mr. Van Matre came to town to look for employment manufacturing musical instruments. He would eventually own a controlling interest in the Schumann Piano Company.

Erma Donnelly Van Matre was born on June 12, 1888, in Chicago and was a member of the Schmauss family. She grew up in a home located on the corner of Jefferson and Main Streets. Erma married Willard in 1911. In 1915, Willard first became interested in the theater business and formed a partnership with James Hurst and T.M. Ellis. During World War I, Willard's business deals were put on hold as he served in France.

It was Willard's idea to build an atmospheric theater here in Rockford.

Willard Van Matre. *From Midway Village Museum, Rockford.*

The Coronado Theater.
*From Midway Village
Museum, Rockford.*

He wanted to give theatergoers a unique experience where they would have a sense that they were in a luxurious outdoor theater. This type of theater offered a wonderful organ, a starry sky overhead and a simulated sunrise using lights and music. The very first theater of this kind opened in Houston, Texas, in 1922.

Willard thought his theater would help the developing downtown area. He was a smart businessman and decided to include seventeen apartments and several stores in the building as well. This, he hoped, would ensure income during slow theater times.

The Coronado Theater was a success even from the opening day on October 9, 1927, when the Coronado hosted over nine thousand guests for three showings of the silent film *Swim Girl Swim*, starring Bebe Daniels. Many celebrities would grace its stage, including Bob Hope, the Marx brothers, Bella Lugosi and Sammy Davis Jr. John Kennedy used the Coronado when he visited Rockford during his campaign for president in October 1960.

Willard and Erma and their partners didn't stop with the Coronado Theater, though. They purchased the Palace Theater in 1933 and the Midway in 1936. In 1938, they built the Times Theater, and in 1941, they built the Auburn Theater in the north end area of town. They called their business Rockford Enterprises Incorporated.

Willard and Erma loved the Coronado so much they decided to locate their home inside the theater by combining two of the proposed apartments. Their apartment is as beautifully designed as the rest of the theater and included a stylish Art Deco look.

Willard didn't fight during World War II, but he assisted in the effort to sell war bonds. He decided to bring movie stars to Rockford for a special event, and during the week that he scheduled the stars, he sold $1 million worth of bonds.

The Van Matres were the perfect hosts, and there are many tales of Willard dressed in a tuxedo to greet guests as they came for performances. Even after he suffered a heart attack in 1952, he would be carried down in a chair so that he could continue to share his beloved theater. Willard died in April 1953, but Erma continued to live in the theater and handle all the affairs until she died in their apartment on March 18, 1969. Erma proved to be a very good businesswoman, and the theater thrived under her care.

Before Erma passed away, she left over $1 million for a rehabilitation center for victims of illness or accidents. The Van Matre Rehabilitation Hospital first opened in 1967 as a part of Rockford Memorial Hospital. "She was the kindest woman who ever lived," said Edward Abegg, Illinois National Bank and Trust Company officer and trustee of Mrs. Van Matre's will.

This was said about both of the Van Matres. They often spoke of how good Rockford had been to them and how they wanted to give back to the community. Erma was dedicated to helping people, especially crippled children. "Her gift will enable thousands disabled by sickness or injury to return to a satisfying and productive life," read a *Register Republic* article on December 6, 1973.

The Coronado Theater was listed in the National Register of Historic Places in 1979. The listing noted, "It is one of the best preserved movie palaces in the country and was at its inception among the finest of its type. The Coronado is a particularly fine example of the 'atmospheric' style of movie theatre pioneered by John Eberson, inspiring the audience to believe that they were enjoying entertainment 'al fresco.'"

Apparently, the Van Matres couldn't bear to leave their wonderful theater even after they passed away. Reports of unusual things happening in the apartment and throughout the theater began shortly after Erma's death. In fact, there are several other entities that seem to want to make sure people know they are still around. There are many reports of strange noises, hearing people talking when there is no one else in the building, smelling perfume and cigars and even spotting full-bodied apparitions. Mr. Van Matre himself has been seen numerous times in different parts of the theater, especially on nights when big performances are scheduled.

Their presence, especially Erma's, is still felt in the apartment that they called home. Erma had a beautiful cabinet that she treasured that is still in the home. Apparently, she does not like it when people touch it and will either blast trespassers with a heavy perfume or a cold draft.

Erma's cabinet stands in the apartment home of the Van Matres. *From author's collection.*

Several paranormal investigation teams have explored the theater with some surprising results. They have recorded some great EVPs and disembodied voices and gotten some interesting readings from different types of equipment. But it is not just ghost hunters who have these experiences. The Land of Lincoln Theater Organ Society (LOLTOS) is a volunteer group that was in charge of the maintenance of the building for many years and still continues to care for the theater. Coronado board members Marty Mangas and Dee Huffstedler help organize the tours and have spent countless hours collecting the Coronado's history.

Members of LOLTOS have experienced many strange incidents over the years. These usually occurred when they were all alone in the building, working on one project or another with the doors firmly locked.

The members are always willing to share the stories of their experiences. Sometimes, they would be in the building, completely alone, and they would spot a person down a hallway. When the member would approach these people, the person would disappear right before their eyes.

One story that the volunteers shared involved a gentleman by the name of Marshall. Marshall worked in the theater reupholstering the seats when the Coronado was closed for remodeling. Marshall was in the theater all by himself many times while he worked on the seats. When he finished for the day, he would gather up his tools and radio to place them on a table so he could grab them in the morning to return to work.

Early one morning, Marshall entered the theater and walked to the table to get his tools and radio to begin work. The items were not on the table where he knew he had left them. He couldn't find them anywhere and left the area to determine where they might be. Marshall calculated later that he was gone for fifteen minutes. When he returned, the tools and the radio were right where he originally left them.

There are a lot of other unique incidents that have been reported at the theater. One legend states that if you stand to face the mirrors in the main lobby that you might catch Mr. Van Matre's reflection in the mirror next to you. If you look to your side, there will be nothing next to you, but when you look back at the mirror, the reflection will show his image.

There have been reports of a formally dressed couple seen dancing across the stage to the sounds of an unseen orchestra. This occurs several times a year and seems to correspond with Erma's birthday and the couple's wedding anniversary.

Other claims include the smell of a heavy, floral-scented perfume that seems to overwhelm people and even clings to their clothing. Volunteers attribute the perfume smell to Miss Kileen, who was an office manager at the theater at one time. Miss Kileen is rumored to be very territorial and protective of the theater.

There was also a stage manager, Louis St. Pierre, whose spirit seems to linger around backstage and in the auditorium. A story that is attributed to St. Pierre happened on an evening after a show when stagehands were cleaning up from a production and one of them decided to throw some dry ice onto the stage, causing it to break and smoke.

Other workers joined in and caused quite a commotion. One worker happened to look up toward the balcony, and there was a man dressed in a very nice suit, scowling at them. Apparently, he did not approve of their actions. They were so frightened by what they saw, the crew decided to finish cleaning up in the morning.

There have been many stories of disembodied voices all throughout the building. One night during a paranormal investigation, a group heard voices coming from the men's bathroom in the lower level. Two members of the group stepped into the bathroom only to discover more adjoining rooms. The two members advanced through the rooms. Every time they thought they would certainly find someone in the room, the sound seemed to move into the next area.

The most curious claim seems to be one of a woman in white. After an event one evening, the facilities manager was securing the theater when he got the feeling he was being watched. He was on the stage and decided to snap a photograph of the seat area. Though he said he did not see the woman with his eyes, he caught her in the photograph. Standing just beyond the doorway of the auditorium, there was a woman in a white dress. When the photograph was enlarged, it was easy to see that she wore her hair in a loose bun.

The same woman has been sighted in many areas in the theater. She is also featured in a story that took place across the street from the theater. On May 19, 2014, Rockford police were called in to check the elevator in the parking garage located directly across from the Coronado Theater. They had received a report from a person living in a neighboring high-rise apartment that someone appeared to be riding up and down in an elevator located in the garage. They described the person as a woman dressed in a long white gown.

Police arrived and sent cars to different floors of the seven-story structure. Officers reported that the elevator was going up and down, but they did not locate anyone inside the elevator.

There have been a couple of deaths in the theater, but research has failed to identify the woman in white. In the late 1920s or early 1930s, shortly after the theater opened, there was a Chinese acrobat act on stage. One of the men was supposed to flip into the air during the act. It all went very well during rehearsal, but for some reason during the actual act, when the man flipped into the air, he hit his head on a hook that was hanging from the ceiling. He died right on the stage.

Volunteers for the theater also tell the story of a woman who passed away during a performance from a heart defect. She was the mother of an infant who was starring as the baby in the Splendor and Majesty Holiday Show. The woman was backstage holding her child, waiting for the cue, when she suddenly collapsed. According to witnesses, she was dead when she hit the floor. Luckily, a man standing next to the woman caught the infant, saving it from injury.

There are also tales of an angry man who is occasionally seen by the volunteers and staff members. They describe the sightings as being similar to a chance meeting with someone who has a nasty temper rather than a dark presence.

Willard and Erma have been gone for many years, but there are many people who believe that they and several other spirits still linger in this very unique location. Some people have voiced their opinion that all these people put their heart and soul into the creation of the place and worked very hard for its success. They suggest that maybe the spirits of the Coronado Theatre are just happy to still be a part of the show.

VETERANS MEMORIAL HALL

LEST WE FORGET

In 1899, the well-known local soldier Thomas G. Lawler, who was the commander of the Grand Army of the Republic (GAR), Garret L. Nevius Post No. 1, submitted a petition to the Winnebago County Board. The petition, signed by two hundred men, was a request for a building specifically for veterans. This building, named the Veterans Memorial Hall, was finished in 1903. It was the first ever of its kind built in Illinois and, according to some sources, the entire United States. Its purpose was to "serve as a constant reminder to all of the sacrifices given by the brave men and women from Winnebago County and a way for generations to remember and learn about their lives."

It has gone through many challenges over the last 113 years, but its purpose has always remained the same, to serve Winnebago County's veterans and their families. The dedication of the building was so special that President Roosevelt himself came to dedicate the building for veterans of all the wars past and present.

This is definitely a building where the walls actually do talk. The walls bear the names of five thousand veterans from Winnebago County who served in the Civil War and the Spanish-American War. The first-floor walls are bordered by the names of Civil War battles. It also contains many actual artifacts from the men and women from Winnebago County who have served in the wars. Many of these priceless items were donated either by the service people themselves or by their families. Each item tells the story of the person to whom it belonged. Many theorize that

Veterans Memorial Hall. *From Midway Village Museum, Rockford.*

this explains the high amount of paranormal activity that has been experienced here.

Several dramatic events have taken place inside the stone walls of the hall. Thomas G. Lawler, the man who fought so hard for the building, was laid in state there before his funeral. Several thousand people came through in the four hours that his body was on display. Most people left with tears in their eyes at the loss of this amazing man.

Another memorial was held there for another remarkable Rockford hero. Mary J. Brainard was a Civil War nurse who followed her husband when he left to serve his country. She wrote poetry that told of the devastation she witnessed during those years.

Other stories echo in the building that are harder to decipher but just as deeply imprinted upon the hall. Many people have seen a woman walking on different floors. This author has even seen her, though I did not realize she was an apparition at the time. I was waiting outside the door that opens onto Main Street for the manager to unlock the door. As I was starting to wonder if I should knock again, I saw a woman dressed in a long gown descending the stairs. I thought maybe she was there assisting the manager, so I knocked on the glass. The woman never turned to look at me as she walked down the stairs to the first floor and turned the corner to continue down to the basement. I was really annoyed by this time, and when the manager let me in a few minutes later, I shared the story and told him that the young lady was very rude to completely ignore my knockings. The manager had a strange expression on his face as he told me that he was alone in the building.

Paul Smith, one of the psychics who have assisted with Haunted Rockford events, thinks he knows the woman's identity. Other psychics have validated Paul's impression of the woman's story over the years. The woman was coming to receive the travel information for her young son who was returning home from the army for Christmas. When she came to the hall for the information, she received one of the dreaded telegrams that began with the words that everyone with a loved one in the armed services fears: "We regret to inform you that your son has been killed." The impression of her agony in that moment still continues in this historic building. It seems to linger especially around one of the benches. People who have sat on the bench have described their feelings of overwhelming sadness.

Paul was able to fit the pieces together at another event, this time at the Cedar Bluff Cemetery, when he solved the mystery of the woman's identity. We were also joined by another psychic, Sara Bowker, for that event. I research all of the stories and never tell Paul or Sara before the tours which people we will be speaking about. Usually they walk a distance away and discuss their impressions with Paul's wife, Lisa, who writes everything down for them. While they are doing this, I am telling the story of the person to the group.

I had not even begun my story when Sara immediately started to share her impressions with the group. Sara explained that she had a young man who was communicating with her. He shared his experience of being on the battlefield in France. The man told Sara that the field was covered in mustard gas and that originally he was wearing a gas mask. This man turned to see where his best friend was and was horrified to see his friend had been wounded and was on the ground. The man removed his own mask and rushed to place it on his friend. He then picked his friend up and carried him to safety. Unfortunately, he could not save his friend, and he himself became ill from the gas. The young man was distressed that he left something behind and he was desperate to tell Sara and Paul his story.

While Sara was sharing her impressions, I could see that Paul was also communicating with the young man. Paul stated that the young man kept saying, "You know me. You know me and my mom." Suddenly, Paul said, "His mother is the woman at the Veterans Memorial Hall who went to receive her son's travel information and instead found out that he had died." Paul was so overwhelmed by the feelings that the son and mother had both shared with him that he needed to take a break from the tour.

Damon and Della Grant's headstones mark their graves at Cedar Bluff Cemetery. *From author's collection.*

The young man's name was Grant Damon, and his mother was Della. Grant's death occurred just as he described it to Sara. He had been injured by the mustard gas while in France, and he suffered for a month before succumbing to the effects of the gas. Grant had been dead a month before word reached home to his family. Some people may not believe in psychics or that spirits can communicate with us, but I can tell you that everyone on the tour believed it that evening.

Other paranormal claims in the Veterans Memorial Hall are of children who were kept in the balcony area during meetings and a band that plays on as though still celebrating happier times. There is also a couple who sit on the far side of the balcony. Paul and Sara shared that this couple was attending a funeral there and were not pleased that there were children running around at such a stately event.

Some of the experiences that people have shared at the hall may be what is known as residual hauntings. These are the type of hauntings that take place almost like a loop of video. It plays over and over, and there is no connection that can be made between the observer and the participants. One example would be the woman whom I saw while at the door. She walked down the stairs and never even looked my way even though I was pounding on the door to attract her attention.

Other experiences could definitely be classified as intelligent hauntings. These incidents occur while conducting investigations. The person is attempting to connect with the spirit by asking questions and using a digital recorder or a flashlight to signal a response.

This location seems to have its share of both types of hauntings. There have been several investigations conducted in the building, and EVPs have been recorded during these that indicate that something paranormal is happening. Other incidents have included people seeing shadows and hearing music and footsteps going up and down the stairs.

This unique building is considered by many to be sacred ground. It is a place where the men and women of our county and the sacrifices they made for their country are still remembered and where their legacy is passed on to new generations. The current manager, Scott Lewandowski, has worked very hard to offer events

The Veterans Memorial Hall. *From author's collection.*

to ensure that these men and women will not be forgotten. The hall has recently been granted permission to have a statue that features a Civil War soldier moved to the Wyman Street entrance. The soldier once stood on the old courthouse lawn and most recently stood at the intersection of Main and Auburn Streets on the grounds of Greenwood Cemetery. It seems a fitting memorial to all who served and those who currently serve in our armed forces.

THE TINKER FAMILY GHOSTS

Tinker Swiss Cottage Museum and Gardens is a beautiful mansion tucked away on Rockford's west side. Quite a few Rockfordians know it is there, and some of them even know its history. What might surprise people is that the cottage has the reputation of being haunted.

The house is a very unique place for several reasons. It is located on a limestone bluff overlooking the Kent Creek, and there are signs of a definite Native American presence. Water, limestone and Native American influence are all said to be great conductors of paranormal activity.

The bluff is located just above where Germanicus Kent, Lewis Lemon and Thatcher Blake landed when they decided to settle this area. It is definitely an important spot in Rockford's history, both good and bad. The Tinkers sold the land to the railroad, and one of the area's first cemeteries was once located across the creek from the cottage. The bodies were supposedly moved when the railroad was built. Rumors persist to the contrary, however. These stories state that when family members could not be found, the bodies were left there and the tombstones removed.

The area around the railroad was also a place of violence during the 1920s and 1930s, when there was a large amount of transient traffic as men traveled from place to place looking for jobs. It was right in the middle of the action during Prohibition, and there have been many unfortunate souls that came to a bad end in the area.

But the cottage rests above it all. It is filled with the Tinker family's possessions. This is not a house that has been decorated with pieces brought in from sales or donations. The Tinker family not only gave the Rockford Park District their house but also included all of their possessions, creating a time capsule of the era they lived there. They left clothes, dishes, diaries and furniture. This could be another reason why there is so much paranormal activity here.

The cottage was built by Robert Tinker and his wife, Mary. Mary's first husband was John Manny, who, along with his cousin John Pels Manny, built the Manny Reaper Company. John died young from tuberculosis, and Mary, an extraordinary

Robert Tinker. *From Tinker Swiss Cottage Museum, Rockford.*

The Tinker Swiss Cottage. *From Midway Village Museum, Rockford.*

Mary Dorr Manny Tinker. *From Tinker Swiss Cottage Museum, Rockford.*

woman for her times, decided to take over the company after his death.

Mary and Robert Tinker met when he came to work for her company. Robert traveled to Europe, and it was there that he first saw the Swiss chalets that he would use in the design of his own unique home. Mary and Robert eventually fell in love and were married.

Robert served as mayor for a year and also became involved in the Rockford Park District. He was a master gardener and surrounded his lovely home with winding paths and beautiful flower gardens. He also built a suspension bridge across Kent Creek to connect with Mary Manny's grand mansion. After they sold that property to the railroad, Robert designed gardens for the train passengers to stroll through while they waited for their connecting trains.

Mary and Robert had no children of their own, but they did open their home up to several of Mary's relatives. Josephus Dorr, Mary's father, became ill and came to stay in the upstairs of the home. It was here that he drew his last breath. Mary's nieces Marcia and Jesse Dorr came to live with the couple as they attended the Rockford Seminary. Marcia would die in the home, and in 1901, Mary herself became ill and passed away in the house. Hers was one of the several funerals that were conducted in the parlor of the home. Robert designed a very impressive monument for Mary in Greenwood Cemetery in 1902.

Robert and Jesse were left in the home. During this time, a single woman and a man could not live in the same place, so as a matter of convenience, they were married. Jesse devoted her life to helping orphans and would eventually adopt a young son for her and Robert to raise. They named him Theodore. Robert died in 1926 and Jesse in 1942. Jesse gave the house and all of its furnishings to the Rockford Park District to be used as a museum.

Haunted Rockford has visited this unique place for several years now and has enjoyed working with Steve Litteral, the executive director. Right from the very first tour, people had experiences they could not explain.

The first time we ever visited the cottage on one of the Haunted Rockford bus tours, we were joined by a paranormal investigation team. We split the guests up into small groups, and different guides led them through the cottage. As we were loading the bus to head to the next stop, one of the ladies approached me. She told me that she had really enjoyed the tour. She loved that we used psychics, that we shared the history of the house, that we had the team along and that we had the lady dressed in clothes from the time period of the

Jesse Tinker. *From Tinker Swiss Cottage Museum, Rockford.*

Tinkers. This last piece caught my attention, and I asked her what she meant. She explained that when her group was going out on the suspension bridge, they passed a woman with her dark hair in a bun and all dressed in white.

By now we had been joined by others on the tour, and there was a surprised gasp from several of the members when I explained that we had no one dressed up in a white dress. I wasn't sure who the lady saw, but this mystery woman was not part of the tour. I can't adequately describe the look on the woman's face, but I can tell you that it was priceless.

That first encounter was a definite omen of things to come. Almost every time we have organized an event there, people have experienced something. One other time when we were there with a group, we were upstairs in the "red room" talking about Josephus Dorr, when all of a sudden we heard a woman's voice from downstairs calling, "Hello?" I turned to Steve and asked if he had locked the doors behind us, and he stated that he had. I told him he better go make sure because we were all upstairs and someone must have come in.

Steve had a very funny look on his face when he joined us a few minutes later. He had checked the doors and found they were locked. He searched the entire downstairs, and there was no one else in the building with us. Everyone who was there that night confirmed that they heard the voice.

I had another rather startling experience in the cottage. I was going into the house during one of our public investigations to make sure all was well. I entered the basement from the outside door and was speaking to Sara Bowker, one of the psychics who assist with Haunted Rockford Events. She was explaining to me that there was a ghostly servant girl that was rushing up and down the stairs, apparently trying to serve dinner. As she said this, I was standing at the bottom of the stairs that went between the basement and the upstairs kitchen, and I saw movement from the corner of my eye. I turned to look up the stairs and saw the back portion of a lady in a long blue-patterned dress. I was quite startled and turned to look at Sara. She asked, "Did you see her?" I was astonished and must have shown it because my expression made Sara laugh.

At another paranormal investigation, there was a team member who happened to be in the basement. Mr. Tinker did not seem to like this person. I'm not sure if he was using provoking methods, but toward the end of the evening, one of the participants caught a very clear EVP on his digital phone. I heard the voice recording minutes after this incident took place. The hair on my arms raised when I heard a man's voice clearly state, "Get out."

There have been many incidents reported since by guests. They have heard children playing, been touched, noticed whistling and humming, and seen many full-bodied apparitions. In fact, the cottage has so much activity that it was featured on the *Ghost Hunters* show a couple of years ago.

During a tour right around Halloween, we had a number of people on the second floor. Steve Litteral was in Robert Tinker's room while I was in what is now called Mary Tinker's room. Suddenly, the lights shut off, and we were plunged into complete darkness. I had been co-hosting events in the building for years at this point and this had never occurred before. Steve went down to the basement in an attempt to determine what had happened. There were several members from a paranormal team attending the tour with their equipment. One of the young ladies that had joined us for the tour suddenly started to scream. I was in the same room and tried to maintain calm as I questioned her about what she was experiencing. She stated that something had touched her. I turned my flashlight on and saw that she was alone in the corner, eliminating the possibility of someone from the group having touched her.

It was at this moment that the lights came back on, and the girl stepped away from the corner she had been standing in. The investigators moved in with their equipment to see if they could detect any unusual readings. One of the men held an EMF detector, and when he stepped into the corner, his meter went off to indicate that something was causing the electromagnetic field in the room to spike higher. Some investigators believe that spirits manipulate energy in order to communicate and that these EMF detectors will signal when that is happening. Though most of the other participants were thrilled by the experience of that evening, the young girl was so shaken that she left the tour immediately.

The Tinker cottage has developed quite a reputation for being haunted over the years. Steve Litteral still offers many events and invites Haunted Rockford to attend quite frequently. The paranormal investigations hosted for the public are always popular events and allow everyone who attends the chance to work with different paranormal teams to experience an actual investigation.

Some of the events have included psychics, and they all seem to agree that the Tinker family is still as much a presence today as ever in this home they were so proud of. There were no murders or suicides that took place here. They are just a family who loved their home and who still continue to occupy it.

They can get a little nasty when they are ready for their guests to leave, however. There have been reports of them throwing items at people. One story involved a young man who was in charge of a paranormal team at the time this story took place. He was exploring different techniques for this particular investigation. One thing he did prior to the start of the investigation was place several pennies around on different surfaces. Only he knew the year that was displayed on each of the pennies. He did this to ensure that no one else could sabotage his experiment.

He was investigating all alone in the house and decided to use some provoking techniques. He began making some not very polite comments about the family and their home while walking around in the downstairs portion of the library. Suddenly, he got a feeling that he was no longer welcomed in the room or the entire house, for that matter. He decided that it might be a good time for a break and walked through the house to leave by the kitchen door. Just as he reached the door, a penny sailed into the wall right by his head. He stated later that he scooped up the penny and tried to open the door. It didn't open for a minute, and all the time, a heaviness was filling the room. By the time he got the door open and made it outside, he was very unsettled and shaking. He claimed that even though he did not normally smoke, he asked one of his teammates for a cigarette.

Robert Tinker's library. *From Midway Village Museum, Rockford.*

When he checked the date on the penny that flew at his head, he discovered it was the one he had placed in the upstairs portion of the library. The penny had somehow traveled down a flight of stairs and around several corners

Tinker Swiss Cottage today. *From author's collection.*

before slamming into the wall next to his head. Steve Litteral no longer allows provoking techniques to be used during investigations. He too has had several of his own experiences that he cannot explain. These experiences are usually playful in nature, except for a few times after an event. Steve explains to people now that when they are rude or disrespectful to the family members, they have a way to let him know they are not pleased.

Doors have been slammed in his face, and some nights, long after Steve has left and gone to bed, the alarms will go off in the house. Steve has to drive the forty minutes in all types of weather to meet the police to walk through the house to make sure that all is safe and sound. That is only funny once, according to Steve.

The Tinkers did so much for Rockford between their business and other pursuits. Their unique house still brings travelers to Rockford over 150 years after it was built. The fact that their spirits linger inside these walls is definitely a story worth sharing. I am often asked which haunted place in Rockford is the most active, and I have to say that Tinker Swiss Cottage Museum is definitely one of the top locations. Perhaps Robert himself put it best when he used a quote from a poem of Thomas Campbell on Mary's headstone. It reads, "To live in the hearts we leave behind is not to die."

9

LUCERNE'S RESTAURANT

SPIRITS SERVED HERE

The bright yellow house with purple trim stands out among the other neutral-colored houses on Church Street. The awning also draws the eye to the sign out front that reads, "Lucerne's Fondue and Spirits." While the word *spirits* on the sign is advertising the alcoholic drinks, it could indicate some of the unseen guests that linger here. Mark Tietz, owner and operator of Lucerne's, purchased the building over twenty years ago.

Mark first became involved with the building when the Northern Illinois Hospice Association had its offices in the location. Even back then, he suspected that there was something paranormal happening in the building. It was after he bought the house and decided to use it to pursue his dream of opening his own restaurant that he became absolutely sure.

That was over two decades ago now, and Mark has become quite adjusted to the fact that the house has unseen occupants. "We have had lights go off and on, things moving from place to place, electronics malfunctioning; you name it—it has happened," Mark stated during an interview.

Mark also spoke of one incident when something quite dramatic occurred. The restaurant offers a unique dining experience because of the fondue menu, so it is very popular, especially around certain times of the year. One of its busiest nights is Valentine's Day. Mark had every available staff member on hand, including a new employee. Every available seat was taken, and the girl was quite frazzled as she struggled to keep up with the orders. In the background, Mark's stereo system was playing some nice romantic Frank Sinatra songs. Suddenly, a deep voice boomed, "Get out—

Olin Brouse. *From the Rockford Public Library.*

get out now!" through the stereo speakers. While the other servers and Mark, who have by this time become quite used to such things happening, chuckled and moved on, the new girl was quite shaken by the event. When the other servers explained to her that they had a ghost who liked to play practical jokes during busy times, this young lady was not amused. "She quit on the spot," explained Mark. She told him to keep the money, yanked off her apron and was never seen at the restaurant again.

Mark thinks he knows the identity of the spirits that linger in the building. He believes that the ghosts originate from the family who built the home. The house was built in 1895 by Charles and Anna Utter as a gift for their daughter Lillian and her husband, Olin Brouse. Olin and Lillian were married in 1891, and at first, her parents were not too enthusiastic about their daughter's choice of a mate. Lillian was a beautiful young lady who had made quite a name for herself because of her lovely singing voice. These factors, along with her family's high ranking in the city's social and economic spheres, made her quite an attractive choice for a spouse. This made Charles very careful about any suitor for his daughter's hand.

Olin was a highly respected man who had done well for himself, but he was considerably older than Lillian. This caused her parents to hesitate to give their consent. Lillian must have finally convinced her father because the couple was married in Charles and Anna's home on Court Street in January 1891.

The Brouse family would eventually include a son, Charles, and a daughter named Florence. Olin became ill later in life, and Lillian hired a man to help care for her ailing husband. According to psychics who have visited the home on Church Street, Olin and his caretaker still linger in the home.

While the ghost's activity is usually playful, there have been times when Mark has felt rather startled at some of the incidents. One particular

Lillian Utter Brouse's Headstone in Greenwood Cemetery. *From author's collection.*

experience caught him by surprise. He needed to get some paperwork from his desk on a day when the building is usually empty. It was during the summer of 2012, and since the building was closed for a while, the air conditioner was turned up. The inside of the house was very warm when Mark entered.

"It just felt like someone was in the house when I came in," Mark explained. After checking that there were no signs of a break in and all the security systems and locks were in place, Mark noticed that the phone system's light was on. "The phone system has two colored lights. The green one is for outside calls and the red light indicates an internal call. When I checked the phone it indicated that someone was using the phone upstairs." Unsure of what to do, Mark approached the stairs. As Mark stood at the bottom of the staircase, he felt a coldness approach him from behind.

Mark was frightened but more worried that someone was in the house. "I decided I was going up the stairs. I shouted that I was coming up and just as I said the words, the lights suddenly went out." Mark stated that he was frightened and decided that he would retrieve the papers another day.

Mark went on to say that most times he feels that the spirits just want him to know they are still around. There is a standing rack that is used for customers to hang their coats on. The staff has found it in several rooms when they arrive to set up. Its usual place is in the front room, which used to be the master bedroom when the house served as a home. The night crew members always swear that they last saw it in the customary place after cleaning the evening before. But when the early staff arrives, they often find the coat rack moved. This also happens frequently with tables and chairs.

Staff has also heard the sounds of footsteps coming down the staircase that was used for the servants of the home. This seems to take place at all hours of the day, even when the staff is busy with customers. They notice it quite a bit when they are busy because the staircase is small and two people cannot use it at the same time. There have been times when they are busy and running drinks from the first floor where the bar is located to the patrons seated on the second floor. "We will be approaching the staircase to deliver the drinks and hear someone coming down. So we wait until they descend to start up with the order. We will hear the footsteps coming down, but then no one comes around the corner. That can be frustrating when we are busy," Mark shared during an interview.

Mark also shared that he thinks the spirits approve of his restaurant and might have helped somehow with its popularity. According to Mark, every business that has started in the building has had great success. But he has made an arrangement with the ghosts that linger in the building, just in case. "I told them that they can stay here and have the house all to themselves on the days the restaurant is closed. But they have to be nice and not scare me. If they don't, I will cut up the rooms and make it an eight-family apartment house."

So far, that arrangement seems to work. Incidents continue, but they are playful in nature. Mark and his staff have now become accustomed to the fact that Olin, Lillian and some of their servants still linger in the beautiful home.

THE HAUNTING OF HASKELL PARK

Haskell Park has been a part of Rockford almost from the beginning. It was originally platted as the West Side Public Square in the 1830s. The land was given to the city by Dr. George Haskell and his brother-in-law, John Edwards. George Haskell and his family settled in Rockford in 1838. He remained here for twenty-eight years, helping the new city grow. He found a passion in growing fruit trees and was successful for many years.

Haskell Park still remains, though it has seen many changes over the years. Postcards from the late 1800s and early 1900s show a beautiful place with an elaborate fountain located toward the center. Children used the park as a playground and couples would use the benches as a courting place.

The fountain itself became quite newsworthy in June 1902. The newspapers from June 13 tell the story of a man who was passing through the park late one evening. Just as he was passing the fountain, a strange noise caused him to look at the water. There in the moonlight, he saw a sight that nearly paralyzed him with fright. A shadowy, shimmering form seemed to rise from the water. At first, it was a dark mist, but then the man was horrified to see it take on a human shape. Though it had no distinguishing features, he saw what he imagined to be skeletal hands as the specter reached its arms toward him.

This broke the man's paralysis, and he bellowed in fear while he began to run through the park as if the very devil himself was chasing him. He stated in the interview that he didn't slow down until he reached his house.

The man's friends all teased him viciously about the story until others started to experience the same ghostly shape, always reaching out for

Haskell Park's fountain. *From Midway Village Museum, Rockford.*

whoever braved the park late in the evening. Later stories claimed that the spirit eventually freed itself from the fountain and would chase visitors to the boundaries of the park.

The phantom contained no distinguishable features except the hands, which were always described as skeletal. The black swirling mass always originated from the fountain and was said to rise from the water to follow people. As the stories grew, people started to bypass the center of the park. They claimed that they would see the black mass lurking behind the trees inside the perimeter of the park.

Though no one could identify the spirit, there are several possibilities for the haunting. One is the tragic tale of James and Kate French. They were a couple who lived in Rockford in 1896. They were married in 1890 and opened a confectionery shop at the intersection of Green and South Main Streets. James became jealous of his attractive wife, and this eventually led to the breakup of their marriage. Kate left James and moved back into her mother's home on Cedar Street. James attempted to reconcile and seemed to become crazed by Kate's refusals.

On July 20, 1896, Kate left her mother's house to visit a sick friend. James questioned a small neighbor girl who told him the name of the friend Kate went to visit. James knew where the lady's house was, and he also knew that Kate would pass by Haskell Park on her return. James decided to wait for her there. Later, witnesses would testify they saw James pacing back and forth in the park for hours as he waited for Kate. Though at first no one knew the reason why he appeared so agitated, his motive soon became all too clear. When Kate finally did leave her friend's home, James attacked and shot her. Kate escaped him and raced for her life up the street before she ran into a house to seek help. But James pursued her into the home, where their life-and-death struggle ended.

Neighbors were drawn out of their homes by the gunshots and Kate's screams, and by the time James ran from the house, there were over one hundred men waiting to chase him down. They caught up with him at the Rock River.

James was tried for the murder of Kate and sentenced to death by hanging. His execution was carried out on June 11, 1897, in the yard of the Winnebago County jail. James never showed any remorse for killing his wife and even told visitors that he was glad that Kate was dead. Maybe all the energy caused by his hatred for his wife resulted in his spirit wandering the place where he once waited for her.

Another possibility of the haunting comes from the suggestion that Haskell Park lies over a Native American burial ground and the spirits of those buried there can find no rest. Psychics Sara Bowker and Paul Smith first came in contact with these lost souls on a recent bus tour. They both sensed that the spirits that wander the area are looking desperately for the place where their bodies once rested.

Sara Bowker explained that these people were laid to rest here many years ago, and for hundreds of years, they rested in peace. But when the settlers came, they removed the bodies from these once sacred burial grounds. Now their spirits are no longer at rest. Sara stated, "They don't know where to go or what to do. They will be trapped here until something can be done to help release them."

ETHNIC HERITAGE MUSEUM

HOME TO MANY SPIRITS

Sue Lewandowski is the board president for the Ethnic Heritage Museum, and she has a real passion for Rockford History. The Ethnic Heritage Museum is filled with treasures that represent six different ethnic groups that have called southwest Rockford home. It is a real gem for people who are interested in Rockford's history, and it has an added benefit. The 162-year-old building that contains the museum happens to be haunted.

The little museum was started in 1989 by Menroy Mills, who was the director in the beginning and, some claim, its very heart and soul. The museum features different rooms dedicated to each of the six different ethnic groups that settled in Rockford. Even though people of all six cultures did not live in the house, spirits can attach themselves to objects, and there are many personal objects in each room.

Haunted Rockford hosted its first event at the museum in 2012. At that time, Sue was interviewed about the history of the building and the ghostly experiences encountered there. She mentioned feeling someone else in the room, seeing shadows that move and hearing voices.

Haunted Rockford was joined by renowned paranormal investigator and author Dale Kaczmarek from Chicago for the 2012 event. Dale brought his ghost-hunting equipment along. Psychics Sara Bowker and Paul Smith had never been in the building prior to that evening.

Almost immediately, Paul and Sara sensed that the building had been remodeled. They insisted that there was formerly a flight of stairs to the basement, which is now gone. Sue was astonished when we entered the

The Ethnic Heritage Museum. *From author's collection.*

basement and shone a light through a hole in the cement wall. The light illuminated a set of stairs that had been covered up. "I was not aware those were even there," Sue stated.

Sara and Paul felt drawn to the room with the hidden stairs, and both started to sense the presence of a small boy. Kaczmarek brought his digital recorder and a piece of equipment called an Ovilus to the basement. He and Sara Bowker conducted an EVP session. Several people were present in the basement watching Sara and Dale work. Sara was talking to the little boy that she and Paul had sensed while Dale was observing the equipment. The temperature in the basement dropped several degrees, and then a voice coming from the Ovilus said, "Mark." Dale rewound the digital recorder and replayed it. Right before we heard the electronic voice from the Ovilus saying, "Mark," there was a little child's voice that said, "Come out, come out." Everyone in the room was shocked because they had not heard any voice except Sara's asking questions and the Ovilus. The child's voice was very clear and several witnesses later claimed that the recording made their hair stand up on the back of their necks. Dale also realized that the name Mark came through as a response to Sara's question "What is your name?"

Haunted Rockford has been back to the museum many times since that night, and Paul and Sara have been able to communicate with Mark a little more each time. "It's like he's playing hide-and-seek with us," explained Sara. At first, the team was afraid Mark was trapped in the building after death, but after getting more information from him, Paul and Sara are certain that Mark lived in the house but did not die there.

There are plenty of other spirits that are still in the house, however. The staff experience noises, voices and shadows in many of the rooms. In the Polish room at the front of the house, Paul Smith sensed an older woman who sits in a rocking chair by the front window. He stated that when he feels her there and looks out of the window, he sees a streetscape from a different time period. He also feels that she lets staff know she is there by moving articles around. There is a doll that is dressed in traditional Polish festival clothing, and this particular spirit likes to keep the staff at the museum scratching their heads by moving that doll from place to place around the room.

Another thing that the psychics picked up is that some of the cultures that are represented inside the house are not exactly happy with the other cultures. Apparently, if the cultures clashed in life, this can continue into the afterlife. The staff of the museum is adamant, however, that all of the cultures that were pivotal to Rockford's history will continue to be represented.

12

EMMA'S HOME

Emma Jones was born in Orfordsville, Wisconsin, in 1879, one of sixteen children. Emma and her husband, Frank, were married in Rockford in 1898. The newlywed couple moved around a little. Frank worked as a blacksmith, town marshal and game warden. Eventually, the couple moved into a lovely home not far from the Rock River on the city's east side. The house was built in the mid-1880s and was very distinctive.

Frank owned a transportation company at 117 Madison Street and traveled quite a bit for his work. He grew the trucking company from one single truck into a whole fleet of sixty-two trucks. They had two sons, Carl and Ray. Ray worked with his father to run the transfer company.

Emma had her dogs to keep her company while Frank was away. The dogs were devoted to her and would follow her everywhere. She spent many hours caring for their large home, and neighbors would often give her compliments about the beautiful property. It was easy to tell that Emma truly loved her house. Neighbors would often see Emma puttering in her yard or sitting up in the attic window, watching the boats on the river.

Time passed, and on a cold December morning at the end of 1941, Emma was heartbroken to find Frank dead in their bed. The family held his funeral in the beautiful home. Emma was left all alone in the big house. She still had her beloved dogs by her side and still liked to sit in the attic window, though the view was now blocked with other buildings that had sprung up over the years.

Emma suffered another tragedy when her son Ray died unexpectedly at the age of fifty-nine. The papers told of the kindness and generosity that Ray extended as the head of the transfer company. He moved all the equipment from the old location of the Rockford Memorial Hospital without charge. "His helpfulness crossed religious, social, and economic lines," claimed the *Morning Star* article of December 30, 1962.

Emma couldn't care for the house as well in her advanced years, and it fell into a state of disrepair. Her precious dogs passed away and her grasp on reality started to slip. Her son Carl became concerned and decided his mother shouldn't live alone anymore. He moved her to his home. Her confusion worsened, and she did not understand

Emma Jones House. *From author's collection.*

why she was not in her lovely home anymore. Legend tells that sometimes, Emma would wander away from Carl's home and make it back to her house. She couldn't go in, of course, and her concerned neighbors would see her wandering the grounds and call Carl to come.

The family finally had to admit that Emma would not be returning to the house that she and Frank had shared, and they made the painful decision to sell the home. One of the first realtors to show the place brought a young couple to the home. He realized that the electricity wasn't working, so he made his way into the basement to check the fuse box. The man didn't have a flashlight with him, so he lit a match. In the flickering light of the match, he was startled to see an elderly woman standing next to him! The match went out, and when he finally got another one lit, the woman was gone. The realtor

Jones family monument at Cedar Bluff Cemetery. *From author's collection.*

hurriedly checked the fuses and got the lights to come on. Of course, he never mentioned the woman in the basement to the couple waiting upstairs.

The couple purchased the home and worked very hard to restore it to its former glory. They were slightly concerned with some of the strange things that happened around the house. They often heard the sound of a dog's claws on the hardwood floors and the sound of pieces of metal rattling. They also heard strange knocking sounds all through the house. The couple had exterminators come check for mice, but no reason for the knockings could be found.

One cold February day, the young couple walked into the front parlor and found a little old lady standing there. She looked at them quite cross and demanded to know why they were in her house. They stood there in shock as she walked past them and went out the front door.

They mentioned the visit to the neighbors, who told them it was probably Emma. They explained that Emma was confused and didn't understand that the house was no longer hers. They told the couple to phone the family to let them know that Emma had wandered away again. When the couple called, they were stunned when the family replied that it could not have been Emma who visited them. Emma had died weeks before. The couple moved out shortly after that.

The next man to own the house didn't stay long either. He would receive phone calls in the middle of the night. At first, no one responded to his greetings. But finally, one night when he answered the phone, a voice asked him, "Am I dead?" The voice, he claimed, belonged to an old lady. He also left the house.

Emma Jones Home. *From author's collection.*

After that, the house stayed empty for a while, and the neighbors would speak of seeing someone sitting up in the attic window, the same windows where Emma often sat to wait for Frank.

Emma's house was eventually bought by Meld, a not-for-profit organization that assists teen mothers. Remodeling was done to create office spaces. During the construction, workers had quite a few incidents with the house. When they stepped outside to take a break, the door would lock by itself behind them. They would turn off all the lights when they left for the evening and walk out to the back, where there was a parking area. When they glanced back up at the house, the lights would all be lit again.

The reports of strange incidents didn't stop when the remodeling was finished, however. The ladies in the offices would complain about items turning up missing only to be found in some remote place. They had a little tradition of baking cakes to celebrate the birthdays of the women who worked in the building. The women would leave the cake in the kitchen area on the counter, and several times, they later found that a hunk had been removed from the center. After discussing it, they decided that if Emma were truly still there with them, they should be more accommodating. So they started to cut a piece of cake and leave it there for Emma. After that they never had trouble with baked goods again.

Women working in the building also told of strange noises and decided that it was Emma's dogs. They supposed that it was the dogs' claws and the metal on their collars that were making the noises. They never felt frightened, but they were startled at times. One young lady who was often the last to leave in the evenings told of one night when she left very late. She turned out the lights, locked the doors and set the alarm. She got into her car and was driving past the front of the house when, for some reason, she turned to look at the doorway. There is a large window in the front door, and through the glass, she saw a little old lady standing on the staircase. She didn't stop and go back inside. She said she knew exactly who it was.

Later, the house was remodeled and turned back into a home. It is now owned by a nice family who has really made it into a beautiful home once again. They say that they have never experienced any strange incidents since they moved in. Maybe Emma approves of the house she loved belonging to a family once again.

HOPE AND ANCHOR PUB

WHERE THE SPIRITS ALWAYS LINGER

The Hope and Anchor English Pub can boast the title for "one of Rockford's Oldest Restaurants," especially now that Maria's is closed. It also is one of the most haunted, at least according to owner Kreena Robbins. Kreena and her husband, Ian, have been the owners for almost seven years now, and they really embrace the fact that their place is haunted.

The Robbinses purchased the old Mayflower Restaurant, which had claims to fame for fine dining since the 1930s. Eddie Armstrong owned the restaurant back in the spring of 1936, coming here from Beloit, where he ran the 613 and the Butterfly Clubs. The restaurant during Eddie's time was known for the steaks and the orchestra for dancing. Delbert White ran it in the 1940s, and it became very popular with the social clubs to hold their meetings and business luncheons there.

Anthony Salamone bought the Mayflower from Ted Roell and Bud Flodin in 1968, though, according to Kreena, that may not be what really happened. Flodin and Roell purchased the restaurant in June 1968 and, less than six months later, turned it over to Salamone. The story is that Tony won the restaurant in a card game.

Food must have been in the Salamone blood. Tony's family came from a small village on the outskirts of Venice, Italy. They moved to Rockford in 1911, and Carl, the father, had the idea to open up a delicatessen shop in the front of his home on Kent Street. He sold spaghetti, fresh and dried fruits and dried meats. He wanted to expand and started to sell fresh meat for much cheaper than the other markets around. The shop was very popular, and the family was able to purchase a store in 1914 at 1210 South Main Street. By 1922, they had five different markets throughout the city.

The whole family was very successful, and whether Tony bought or won the restaurant, he continued the tradition of his family. But that success seemed to end after Tony's ownership ceased. In fact, the Mayflower went through so many owners and financial problems that people started to say that it might be cursed. Between the years of 2004 and 2009, the restaurant had seven different owners and a few different names. Kreena and Ian have set up a display to honor the history of their establishment and Tony's memory, and they think that this has helped them.

Kreena and her husband, Ian, knew there was something unique about their location almost from the very start. They heard footsteps going up and down the stairs and then the sound of someone pacing in the office area above the bar. They would store extra glassware in a basement room, but every day when they went down to get some, they would find glasses broken on the floor. Kreena explained, "We don't keep them down there anymore."

People who knew Tony Salamone when he was alive always mention that he loved to play tricks on people. He also liked women, especially attractive blondes. Apparently, according to psychics Paul Smith and Sara Bowker, he still does. Sometimes, if there is a blonde in the women's room, Tony might pull their hair or, if she is really lucky, according to Kreena, he might swat her backside. There is now a chair in the bathroom for the spirit to use.

Another story that the staff has shared involves the upstairs office. This area is behind the public use room upstairs. It definitely has a different feeling from the rest of the building. Apparently the room was once the office for the owners. Female staff members don't like to go into this room because they claim they feel as if they are not welcome there. Psychics Paul Smith and Sara Bowker both experienced the feeling that some shady business might have been carried out in the room. Though they can't tell exactly when this might have happened, they theorize it was probably during the early 1930s and '40s. "Women were not part of these dealings," Paul Smith stated.

The psychics also had the impression that someone might have gotten hurt as a result of a business deal gone wrong. They did not feel that the person died in the office; however, there was a confrontation, and someone was possibly stabbed. This claim has yet to be validated by research.

One staff member who was in charge of the early morning preparation work would come into the restaurant earlier than anyone else. She sometimes would bring her little daughter in with her. While she was setting up the place, her little daughter would entertain herself with the books and toys she brought along from home. Sometimes the little girl would talk to herself and even hold conversations. The staff member just assumed she was talking to an imaginary friend.

The daughter got older and stopped coming in as often. One day the staff member heard her daughter talking in her room at home. She went in to check on her and asked the daughter who she was talking to. The little girl explained that Tony had come to see her at their house because he missed her, and she hadn't visited the restaurant in a while.

The staff member stated that she never shared the previous owner's name with her daughter, and she had no explanation of how her daughter knew that information. She did share that her daughter was never frightened by the visits and even seemed to enjoy Tony's company.

There are also tales of someone playing tricks on people in the bathrooms. Sometimes when the owners are there early or late, after their guests are gone, they would hear the sound of the faucets turning on. Paul and Sara believe that this is the spirit of a little girl. She appears to be about six to seven years old, has long brown hair and spends time by the staircase to the second floor. She likes to play tricks on people by turning the faucets on and off. No one seems to know why she is haunting the Hope and Anchor. She just seems to enjoy the attention.

One thing is certain, whether you come for the unique menu, great music or, if you are really bold, for the ghosts, you are sure to get more than you ever expected at the Hope and Anchor English Pub.

DER RATHSKELLER

A GERMAN FAMILY'S LEGACY

The Der Rathskeller Restaurant on Auburn Street has been known for its tasty food and unique atmosphere since the 1930s. Many people have visited the beautiful biergarten since its addition in 2009. This place is a wonderful combination of Rockford's German history and the present-day quest for good German food and beer. What may surprise some people is that it also houses a few spirits of the paranormal kind.

The history of Der Rathskeller goes back to the early 1930s. Fred Goetz, a Merrill, Wisconsin native, came to Rockford when he was drafted in World War I. Fred was German himself and didn't want to fight in the European campaign against his fellow countrymen, so he was listed as a conscientious objector and served his time at Camp Grant as a quartermaster corps sergeant. He fell in love here, first with his soon to be wife, Irma, and then with the city itself.

Fred decided to settle here after the war and worked for a time as a Burroughs Adding Machine Company salesman. Fred loved the Rockford area, but there was one thing he missed about Wisconsin—good sausage! He searched in vain for the kind of sausage that he had enjoyed as a child, but that did not stop the industrious Fred. Fred decided that if Rockford didn't have it, then he would bring it here. He ordered the sausage from Milwaukee, first for himself and then, as word spread, for his friends. The idea took off in a big way, and by 1931, Fred was ordering sausage for eight hundred households! Fred was a smart man and decided that he would open his own shop.

Fred gave up his job selling adding machines and began to sell meats at his own Sausage Shop on Auburn Street. He sold other things besides sausage, including breads, caviar and cheeses. Fred noticed that many people would buy his sandwiches and stand outside to eat them, so he decided to expand. He set up a couple of tables with some chairs for his patrons to enjoy their food. Before long, he had to expand into the basement, and with a nod to his German heritage, Der Rathskeller was opened.

Rockford's population swelled during the World War II years, and Fred and Irma's little place grew with it. They introduced other foods, including the lyonnaise potatoes, which would become one of the signature dishes. Fred also added imported beers to complete the German experience. In the 1980s, a false wall was discovered in the basement dining area. The stories claim that Fred just might have used this space to hide the illegal liquor that was offered for purchase during Prohibition.

Tragically, Irma was killed in a horrendous car accident on January 3, 1947. What made the accident even worse was that their daughter, Lucy, was driving the car. Lucy was home from her studies at Purdue University, where she was majoring in home economics. Lucy and her mother were in a car traveling south on North Second Street. The roads were very icy, and Lucy lost control and skidded into a fifteen-ton semitrailer carrying a load of grain. Both Irma and Lucy were thrown from the car. Unfortunately, Irma landed in the direct path of the truck and died instantly from crushing trauma to her head. She and Fred had been married for over twenty-six years at the time of her death. Irma's funeral was held at Burpee Underwood Funeral Home, and she is buried at Greenwood Cemetery, located directly across the street from the Der Rathskeller Restaurant.

Lucy was also badly hurt and required a nurse for a while. Lucy's nurse, Bertha Ritter, and Fred fell in love and were married in February 1948. Bertha would also help Fred in the restaurant business.

Der Rathskeller passed into other family members' hands until it was finally sold in 1976 to Betty Giesen; her husband, Dick; and her son, Michael Du Pre. They have continued with Fred's vision, selling their own homemade sausages as well as Usinger brand meats.

Fred loved owning his restaurant, and from staff accounts, he is still there making sure that Der Rathskeller continues in good hands. Staff members have experienced enough odd incidents to make them believe that Fred is still around.

Waitstaff have experienced many subtle things that they describe as almost playful. One incident involved a young girl who worked as a hostess.

She heard the stories of Fred from the other staff and then started to experience them for herself. Once when she was working in the basement dining area, she noticed a napkin that had come unrolled on a table. She stopped to fix it and then went on with her original task. A few minutes later, she passed by the table again, and the napkin was unrolled once more. She thought that the other staff members were playing a joke on her but when she questioned her co-workers, she found they were all up in the main floor dining area. There was no one else downstairs at that time.

Other staff have reported the sound of footsteps while they are downstairs. They would hear them and run upstairs to check to see if someone had entered the restaurant, but no one would ever be there.

Mike Du Pre, son of owner Bette Giesen and now manager of the restaurant, has had a few experiences of his own. These usually occur late at night after Mike has closed the place. He has seen shadows and once even heard his name called through speakers that were turned off. That particular incident startled him so much that he immediately locked the door and left the building.

Paul Smith and Sara Bowker gave their impression of who exactly might be playing these tricks on the staff. They picked up three different entities. The playful prankster seems to be old Fred himself. He just loved the place and is very happy with the changes that have been made. Paul and Sara claim that he just wants the owners to know he is still there.

The other spirits appear to be Fred's first wife, Irma, and his second wife, Bertha. Irma is all business and does not like some of the changes that have been made over the years. Her spirit is associated with a cold breeze that swirls through the downstairs dining room. One of the managers named Steve shared the story of a time he was walking through the downstairs dining area when he was suddenly engulfed in an intense cold. He compared it to going into the walk-in freezer. Sara Bowker and Paul Smith both have felt this and attributed this particular claim to Irma. Sara describes Irma as elegant, with her short gray hair worn in curls.

Paul Smith stated that Irma seemed to be upset by some of the changes in the restaurant. She kept asking him, "Where are my cabinets?" Paul Smith also was in contact with the second Mrs. Goetz, Bertha, whom he describes as friendlier than Irma and seems willing to help with whatever is needed. She asked Paul not to forget about her and told him she is very pleased with what the current owners have done with the building.

Fred worked very hard to advertise his business and to bring people to the North Main and Auburn area. The newspapers from his day describe him as a businessman who enjoyed hosting big events. He seemed to especially enjoy the Halloween season. He would always dress up and arrange for the neighboring shops to be open for the children to trick or treat through the stores. He really delighted in being a part of the festivities. It seems that Fred still appreciates the legacy of his restaurant.

The staff at Der Rathskeller seems to have adjusted to the thought that these spirits remain. They feel more comfortable when the entities are playful but not too startling. Mike Du Pre states that though he hasn't had any direct contact with old Fred lately, he always tells him goodnight when he locks up for the evening—just in case.

15

CAVANAUGH'S GHOST

A STRANGE LIGHT

People have always been fascinated by what happens after we die. Thousands of stories have been shared about personal encounters with the other side. Rockford newspapers have reported these experiences since the early 1890s. One of the first written accounts of a personal encounter with a ghostly presence in Rockford occurred in 1891. It started out, as these things sometimes do, as a rumor that spread through the town. The strange thing about this particular rumor of a ghostly presence was that it took place in a church.

Townspeople on the west side of the river reported that they saw a ghostly light in the Second Congregational Church, which at that time was located at the intersection of South Church and Chestnut Streets. Apparently, people would see this ghostly light making its way through the darkened church. They reported this to the police, thinking that someone had broken in to steal something. Police would check the place thoroughly, only to find no one inside.

At first, people reported just observing the light, but as time went on, the light began to be accompanied by the sounds of the organ playing. The vigil became quite a spectacle as more people came to experience the ghostly visitation. Large groups of them waited outside the church for hours every evening just to experience the phenomena firsthand.

This happened so frequently, that one police officer decided that he would solve the mystery. Officer Cavanaugh was a seasoned policeman whose regular patrol area included this particular church. On June 3,

1891, he decided the time had come to finally put these rumors to rest. Cavanaugh theorized that someone was playing tricks on the folks of Rockford, and he was going to prove it.

The officer patrolled the church every fifteen minutes. Hours passed with no results. Officer Cavanaugh was just about to give up when he looked at the church from his vantage point and saw a small flickering light. As Cavanaugh rushed to the front door of the church, he also heard the distinct sound of organ music playing. He let himself inside with the key he had obtained earlier. He was able to see his way clearly by the glow of a strange light, but just as he reached the room where it was located, the light went out. Suddenly, Cavanaugh was left in complete darkness. He used matches until he found the switch for the lights. Determined to prove his theory, the officer searched every nook and cranny of the entire building and found no trace of anyone.

Cavanaugh decided he needed some assistance and went to find the night policeman, Officer Sullivan. The men returned to the church and once again waited for the light to appear. Officer Cavanaugh stationed himself at the front door, and Officer Sullivan went to the back. Cavanaugh entered the church and just like before, as soon as he gained access to the room where the light was shining, it went out. Better prepared, he carried a flashlight this time.

The music continued as Cavanaugh shone the flashlight beam around the room. When he directed the light toward the pulpit, Cavanaugh saw something that almost made his blood freeze. In the dim light of the now shaking flashlight, Cavanaugh saw a young lady, dressed in what he described as mourning clothes, playing the organ. The brave officer stopped in his tracks. The young lady continued to play as she turned to look at him. As their eyes met, the music stopped and the woman disappeared.

Cavanaugh, startled, called out to Sullivan to ask if he had seen anyone. Sullivan answered that he had not. Cavanaugh turned toward the organ and again saw the young lady sitting on the stool. The sight chilled and saddened him at the same time. Cavanaugh rushed to the front door to let Sullivan in, and as they entered the room, the music stopped. The young lady had disappeared.

The two officers searched the entire building and found no one inside and no clue of how the woman entered or left the building. They lingered to see if she would repeat her performance, but the woman did not return. Satisfied that they would learn no more, they left the building. Officers Cavanaugh and Sullivan both claimed that although neither of them believed in spirits, they could find no other explanation for what they heard and saw.

16

FAIRGROUND PHANTOM

Fair Grounds Park was formed on land purchased around 1858 and was used for a variety of activities, including a place to host the annual fair. During the summer of 1896, the Fair Grounds Park made the newspapers for something other than these festivities. The newspapers mentioned that the fairground had become known for its ghostly encounters. At first, the reports just trickled in, mostly told by the closest neighbors to the park. These included stories of mysterious lights, a high-pitched scream that resembled the screeching of a stabbed pig and loud cracks that sounded like revolver shots.

The stories soon expanded to include reports of wispy figures darting in and out of the cattle shed and the halls of the buildings on the grounds. As the stories started to spread through the city, the numbers of the nightly visitors grew. They were all anxious for a glimpse of the apparition.

Eventually, a group of young boys banded together to investigate the claims of the supernatural sightings. The first night, just a handful of boys showed, but soon, the number had swelled to over fifty. They were from neighborhoods from all over the city and differed in age, ethnicity and financial backgrounds.

These amateur ghost hunters had little equipment except for lanterns. The local papers later stated that the boys did arm themselves with everything from toothpicks to telegraph poles. They hoped to use these items to protect themselves from whatever was lurking behind the high fence of the park.

Almost immediately, the boys were startled by a sound much like a shot of a revolver and then the screeching that was described as an unearthly, inhuman sound. This excited the group and bolstered their courage enough to enter the shadowy recesses of the park itself. Their search of the grounds was in vain, however, and the group quickly grew bored with the hunt. It was about this time that a trolley passed by the entrance and attracted the attention of the group.

The band of boys started to hoot and holler, sounding very much like the reported banshee from the park. This startled the trolley occupants nearly half to death. The noise from the group also roused the neighbors, who then came to see what the commotion was all about. Someone finally alerted the police to all this noise, and they arrived in short order. The police had no real idea what was happening but very quickly got the neighbors and would-be ghost hunters under control. They eventually arrested twenty-eight boys from the group and marched them, double file, to the police station.

When they told their story to the judge, he and the spectators in the very crowded room weren't sure what to think. It was the first time Judge Morrison had to make a decision on a case like this. He addressed the crowd of boys, who ranged in age from twelve to thirty years old. Judge Morrison decided to fine the older boys five dollars and gave the younger boys a penance of delivering bouquets to the hospital two times a week.

The police took the ghost claim seriously and spent several nights in the fairgrounds to discover for themselves the cause of the reports. They experienced some of the same things as the claimants. They eventually decided that these were the work of a real, living being and rousted a "semiprofessional hobo" by the unfortunate name of Parrot Face Tompkins. Apparently, the police made sure he would never repeat his performance because Parrot Face was heard to say that he had enough of ghosts (and the police) to last the rest of his days.

17

GHOSTS AT THE GAS HOUSE

Dave Ferguson worked for the gas company located along the Rock River and was very proud of his job. By 1893, he had worked for the company for just over twenty years shoveling coal. He liked the thought that his hard work in the darkened rooms of the gas manufacturing plant brought light to the homes of Rockford.

All that changed in the early months of 1893, when Dave, along with his fellow co-workers, started to fear for their safety while at work. Dave finally had to report some strange occurrences in the plant to his supervisors, and as often happens, the story was leaked to the press. The report stated that the workmen at the gas company were being plagued by what they claimed was a ghost. It started as shadows fliting about the walls of the place. Next, tools were moved about and loud bangs were heard. These were just annoying incidents that did not really frighten the men. Dave was later interviewed by the local newspaper, and he shared that those types of experiences had occurred for some time.

Recently, things had changed, and the alleged ghost began to throw things at the workmen. At first, it was little things, pieces of coal or small tools. It was only after larger items began to sail through the air that Dave and his co-workers became worried.

It would usually begin at around 8:00 p.m. and then continue for hours throughout the men's work shift. The men felt like they were being watched, and several reported that they saw a large shadow blocking out the light from the skylight in the roof. The shadow appeared to watch them from its rooftop vantage point. Then, as the evening progressed, they would begin to see the shadow flitting around the plant's walls. Shortly after these shadows were seen, items would begin to fly through the air. Large chunks of coal and lead pipes were thrown about, and Dave and his co-workers were frightened that they would become injured.

When the men were interviewed, they were asked their impressions of the origin of this apparition. Ferguson, the group's spokesman, stated that he believed that the spirit was of a person who had done something bad in life and was doomed to continue the wrongdoings.

Ferguson also mentioned that all of the men had experienced another apparition that for years walked along the west side of the river. That particular ghost was frightening to behold because it was dressed all in white and was completely headless. It would appear inside the plant on occasion and walk through before it disappeared. It never tried to interact with the workers and certainly never threw objects.

The men believed that the new apparition was trying to harm one of them and that action needed to be taken for their safety. When asked what the supervisors had suggested as a solution for this dilemma, Ferguson just shrugged. "They told us to go find a rabbit's foot for protection." Not just any rabbit foot would work, though. According to the men, the foot must belong to a rabbit that was caught in a church graveyard.

Further research into this story failed to reveal whether this method proved successful, however. There was no further mention of the situation in the local newspapers.

18

THE LEGACY OF ARTHUR BLOOD

Folks around this area who are interested in ghosts and strange happenings eventually take the short drive to Flora township. It is a pretty, rural area with nothing much to see except for crops and farm animals. There is not much there to indicate that this stretch of road is very well known to anyone who is even remotely curious about the paranormal.

There are several legends attached to the road with the unfortunate name of Blood's Point. Though no one seems to remember exactly when these started, most agree that they have been spread for generations. The name may make one think that something tragic happened here. The truth is the road was given the name of the first man who settled the area in 1841, Arthur Blood.

The stories about the road have continued to spread, and now to visit there is almost a rite of passage. Whole carloads of people will drive the road late at night just for the chance that they will witness something supernatural. The stories are much like the stories you hear all over the country. Stories of hellhounds that guard the cemetery, a witch that caused problems for the early settlers and children hanged from a bridge or who died in car accidents have persisted for years.

Mike Rutlin, a former team member of the now disbanded Forest City Paranormal, was interviewed recently. He shared details of an encounter with one of the legendary dogs. Mike was driving down Blood's Point Road one night with a friend. It was a warm evening, and they had the windows down in the car. They heard a strange noise coming from behind. Mike described the sound as similar to metal dragging on the concrete. Suddenly, there was a huge dog's head in the window, growling and barking. "We were probably going over forty miles per hour. This thing came out of nowhere!" Mike stated.

Mike went on to explain that he studies the occult and these large, black dogs are often collectors or the protectors of lost souls. They were near the end of Blood's Point, not far from the cemetery, when the attack took place. Mike theorizes that these dogs guard the area surrounding the cemetery.

Other stories claim that while driving, people were followed very closely by a large black pickup truck. Some tell of their frightening experience of having the car race up behind them, practically blinding them with the bright lights. This truck rides their bumpers, causing them to go faster to get away. Suddenly, the truck will disappear. They believed that the unseen driver of the black vehicle meant to harm them.

Blood's Point also has a story of Beulah, an alleged witch. This story has different versions. One version includes the story of old Arthur Blood. Arthur and his wife were blessed with many children and a large lot of land. They had livestock, and their fields were very productive. They got along well with most of their neighbors, even Old Lady Beulah. She was mean and nasty to the other folks, and everyone called her a witch. The Bloods didn't listen to what the neighbors said, and they let their children play with the old woman, who treated their children well.

Things went along like this until the winter of 1842. No one was prepared for a winter that was very severe and seemed to last forever. One-third of all the livestock in the area died. People suffered horribly. When the spring finally arrived, it brought no relief because fires destroyed all of the crops and orchards.

People started pointing fingers at each other, trying to blame someone for the devastation. The neighbors turned on the Bloods because their children had a relationship with Beulah, whom they suspected had brought these trials to their community. They whispered about the Blood family and spread rumors about the children losing their souls to the devil because of their friendship with Beulah.

At first, Arthur scoffed at these rumors, but after a time, he began to believe them. He was tortured with the thought that his children's souls would be lost. In his desperation to save his children from eternal damnation, Arthur decided that he should kill the children before Beulah could turn them against God. Arthur hanged them from a railroad bridge. It is said on certain nights, when the moon is just right, you can see their little bodies swaying under the train trestle.

In the other version, Beulah takes revenge on the settlers when they blame her for the bad winter and spring. They forced her out of her home. She returned and lured the children out to the woods, where she hanged them. They say Witch Beulah appears in the woods beside the road, accompanied by her black cat, still seeking vengeance against those who harmed her. Her cat will dart out into the road in front of vehicles, forcing them to swerve and crash.

Beulah's hatred has supposedly cursed the whole road, making all sorts of bad things happen. One accident that she allegedly caused involved a van full of handicapped children. The van driver was a lovely young woman who really cared for the children. They had all been to a party, and some of them were still in their costumes from the day, including the driver. She was dressed up in a clown suit with her faced painted with a large smile.

The children had a busy day, and some of them were dozing. It was a long drive, so to keep the others entertained, the driver was singing to them. She often glanced back in the rear view mirror to ensure the children were still strapped into their seat belts. It was during one of these glances that something ran into the road. By the time the driver looked back, it was too late. She turned the wheel to avoid hitting the creature and lost control of the vehicle, hitting the guard rail at high speed. The van went off the road, breaking through the barricade and plunging to the railroad tracks below. Everyone in the van was killed. The driver was horribly mangled from the steering wheel.

The legend goes on to say that the children are still there in the woods, by the stretch of road where the accident occurred. Some people swear they have seen them while others have heard the sounds of children's laughter when they left their car.

The children are supposedly there to help anyone who might have issues with their automobile on that stretch of road. The legend states that if you stop your car on the road and put it in neutral, the ghosts of the children try to help by pushing the car out of danger. Witnesses who have tried this have sprinkled baby powder on the trunk only to find small handprints left in the powder by the ghostly children.

If you do happen to try this and get out of your car to check, you might hear the children's laughter coming from the woods nearby. Sometimes, you might even see their small shadows in those woods or the ghost of the driver, still dressed in her clown suit.

Research has shown some things in these stories are actually true. There actually was an Arthur Blood. His whole family lived here in Boone County in the 1830s. Arthur was the first to settle in the Flora township. He was married, and there was a boy under the age of five in the household. Arthur built his house on a hill there, and it became known as Blood's Point.

There were two families who joined them, the Daniel Bliss and Wait Rice families. They lived in one of the log cabins that Arthur built. Daniel Bliss died in 1846 and was the first person buried in Blood's Point Cemetery. Wait Rice died a couple years later and was buried there, too. Research has not yet found any Bloods listed in the records for that cemetery.

There have been some terrible, fatal accidents along Blood's Point Road, but so far, no research has found one involving a van or bus full of children. Some of the accidents might have been caused by an animal darting across the road, but this was not mentioned in the news accounts.

Most people would have trouble believing any of these claims in the light of day. But each year, new stories of encounters are shared. While research has not discovered the true origins of these stories—other than the unfortunate name, of course—the true mystery might just be why these claims have continued year after year.

ROCKFORD'S FAIR DAUGHTER

Charles Spafford and his wife came to Rockford in 1839. They became well known and highly respected as one of Rockford's founding families. Carrie, their eldest child, was born on December 2, 1843. The Spafford family hosted lavish parties, and Carrie was considered to be a gracious hostess. It was at one of these gatherings that young Carrie met the dashing Elmer Ellsworth. Ellsworth was quite taken with the sixteen-year-old Carrie.

Ellsworth worked in Chicago in a patent office. But his real interest was in being a professional soldier. He was particularly interested in a French military unit called the Zouaves, a predecessor of the French Foreign Legion. They had elaborate and bright uniforms that were very distinctive. Elmer actually studied French to assist him to master the Zouave drills. He then formed his own military unit to travel the country and participate in parades.

Carrie returned Elmer's affections, but this young couple had one

Carrie Spafford. *From the Rockford Public Library.*

formidable challenge in their relationship: Carrie's father. Charles Spafford was a self-made man who had no time for these fancy young men who didn't seem to have any business sense. He demanded that Ellsworth find a more suitable profession if he wanted to pursue Carrie's hand, and since Ellsworth wanted to be worthy of Carrie's family, he went off to Springfield to become a lawyer.

While he was pursuing his new career, he met the young Abraham Lincoln. They became close friends, and when Lincoln won the election in 1861, Ellsworth followed him to Washington. In fact, Ellsworth became devoted to the entire Lincoln family.

Elmer Ellsworth. *From the Rockford Public Library.*

Ellsworth was trained as a real officer, and when the Civil War began, he raised the Eleventh New York Infantry Regiment. While he was away, he often wrote Carrie. One of Ellsworth's letters to Carrie stated, "My own darling Kitty, the highest happiness I looked for on earth was a union with you. Your letters are the only stars in my night of loneliness and trouble."

On May 24, 1861, Ellsworth offered to assist Lincoln by removing a Confederate flag that was hanging in a tavern across the Potomac River in the neighboring town of Alexandria. Ellsworth gathered up a few men, marched over and entered the tavern. They climbed up the stairs, removed the flag and were coming back down when the tavern owner, James Jackson, fired a shot into Ellsworth's chest. He died instantly. One of Ellsworth's companions, Corporal Francis Brownell, shot Jackson dead. Brownell would later be awarded the Medal of Honor. Ellsworth would be the first officer to die in the Civil War.

Lincoln was devastated by the loss of his dear friend. He ordered Elmer's body to be displayed in the White House on May 24, 1861. Thousands of people filed through to look at the face of this hero. Elmer's body was then sent to his hometown of Mechanicville, New York, to be buried.

The news of Ellsworth's death hit all of Rockford very hard. Newspaper headlines from the day mentioned that all of Rockford mourned the loss of this esteemed man who had won the heart of one of the town's fair daughters. There was a special memorial service held to honor the fallen soldier at the Second Congregational Church. Carrie and her family were invited to participate in the funeral, but Carrie was too devastated to attend. She would mourn the loss of her young man for years.

Carrie eventually met and married Frederick Brett. Their wedding in 1866 was a major event in that year's social season. They moved to Boston for ten years and then to Chicago. They had a son named Charles, after her father. Charles grew into a fine young man any family would be proud of. He graduated from Beloit College in 1892 and found a position as a teacher in St. Louis, Missouri.

Carrie probably thought her life of sorrow was over, but she would suffer even greater losses than before. Within a sixteen-month period, Carrie lost her father, her husband and her beloved son. He was only twenty-two and had contracted typhoid.

Carrie spent the rest of her life serving her community, taking a particular interest in the YWCA and in women's issues. She devoted her life to making the lives of women in Rockford better. The Spafford Mansion on Madison Street would eventually be given to the YWCA by Carrie's sister, Eugenia, who was the last Spafford to live in it.

Carrie's work with the community couldn't fill the void in her life completely. Frequently, she would dress in her mourning garb and visit

Carrie Spafford Brett's grave in Cedar Bluff Cemetery. *From author's collection.*

the cemetery where all of her family was laid to rest. Carrie would be seen at Cedar Bluff Cemetery at all hours of the day and night, dressed in her black mourning dress with her beautiful face covered by a veil. Her sobs could be heard all throughout the area of the family plot. People would later call the sight of her heartbreaking as she spent hours kneeling at the graves of her family.

Carrie finally passed away on October 10, 1911. Even after her death, people would still report seeing a woman, all dressed in black in the area of the Brett family stone. Sometimes, she would pass by as others were visiting their family members laid to rest nearby. She never made a sound, but as she passed, the observers would feel a bone-chilling wind swirl by them, even on the hottest of days. These sightings continue today. Others claim that Carrie's sobs can still be heard, seeming to come from all directions at once, filling all who hear the sound with an incredible sadness.

20

A FAMILY'S TERROR

A family living in a haunted house or being visited by a demon isn't a new concept anymore. You can find shows on television almost every night of the week portraying either paranormal investigation teams looking for evidence or a family getting more than they bargained for when they moved into a new house. But when this story took place it was harder to find investigative teams, and most people thought a person was crazy if they claimed to hear disembodied voices.

A book supposedly based on true events was released in 1977. *The Amityville Horror*, written by Jay Anson, was made into a film in 1979. It told the story of George and Kathy Lutz, who bought a house and were forced to flee due to evil forces that threatened to possess them. What some of you might not remember is that Rockford had a case much like the Lutz family's. It took place in 1982 to a family on Rockford's east side.

Vaughn and Sherri moved into what they hoped would be their dream home with their five children. Those hopes were dashed almost a year later when the family fled their home in terror. At first, they tried to ignore what they thought was a ghost, but that ended after the wife, Sherrie, was temporarily possessed by a demon during a séance.

Their claims started shortly after they moved into the home in 1981. The events seemed to appear in a pattern of every three weeks. They heard footsteps walking up the stairs from the basement, after which someone or something would attempt to open the basement door. The television in the living room would turn on by itself in the middle of the night even after the family unplugged it. A ceramic figurine that sat on the organ split straight down the middle as Sherri walked through the living room. Household items, such as pots, pans, plates and silverware, would disappear only to reappear in another location after three weeks. The missing items were always in sets of three. Unexplained foul odors would circulate from the basement. Some of their family members who would stay the night would be awakened at night by the violent shaking of their beds. People who study demons and demonic possessions report similar experiences. They theorize that these occurrences happening in series of three is in an attempt to mock the Holy Trinity.

The incidents grew more frightening until one day when Sherri was visiting with a friend and both of the women heard horrible growling noises coming from the basement. The growls continued as they heard footsteps coming up the basement stairs. Sherri quickly threw herself in front of the door to block it until her friend could wedge a chair under the doorknob. Sherri would later say that someone or something was pushing the door from the other side. Her whole side that was pushed against the door turned extremely cold. Terrified, Sherri and her friend both fled to a neighbor's home. The neighbor insisted on phoning the police despite Sherri's reluctance. The police filed a report that became public, and the newspapers reported on the family's experiences. The police found no explanation for the noises. There was an article that mentioned when the police report was filed, and the officer was startled by the last digits for the case number. The number ended in 666.

Sherri and Vaughn gained the assistance of a local amateur ghost hunter. He offered to conduct a séance with the couple to determine what exactly was in the home. It was during this séance that Sherri seemed to become possessed. Her face contorted and she began to emit a loud growling noise. The men became very frightened for her safety and shook her until she came back to her senses. Sherri had little memory of what had happened during the séance, but she found several deep scratches on her body. The ghost hunter told the family that this was no ordinary ghost and that he believed their house contained a demon.

The family contacted a minister from a local Pentecostal church who agreed to help. The minister agreed to conduct an exorcism but insisted that Sherri leave with the children during the ritual. The minister was joined by his assistant, the ghost hunter and Vaughn. They all stated later in an article in the *Register Star* from March 22, 1982, that they immediately sensed something in the basement. The temperature was colder wherever the presence appeared to be. The men were in the basement for an hour and a half reciting prayers and using anointing oil to cleanse the home. They continued until they felt the presence leave.

The minister came back again to conduct a final prayer service for the family. Though everyone agreed that the presence was gone and the house felt lighter and safer, the family was afraid to remain in the home. They left the house and moved to an undisclosed location. Some people were skeptical about the family's experience while others tormented the family by knocking on their door and requesting to see the demon house. But unlike the Lutz family in *The Amityville Horror* tale, this family was reluctant to go public with the story. One can only hope that their new home brought a feeling of safety for the family.

The *Rockford Register Star* won a third-place award in the local features category for the article that Dave Daley wrote about the incident, titled "The Demon Within." No other claims were found about the family or the location.

21

A RESTLESS SPIRIT

In the fall of 1886, people in Rockford were once again shocked by a very violent crime. The tragedy was made all the worse because the victim was the father of three small children, now left destitute by his death. Besides this aspect of the murder, the newspapers were filled with reports that the murdered man's troubled spirit haunted several places. Rumors claimed that man was so troubled about leaving his family that he couldn't rest in peace.

August Valentine—or Gus, as his friends called him—had no reason to suspect that Saturday would be different from any other day. He worked at Trahern Pump Works, where he was a supervisor over the iron melting department. Gus had been there for fourteen years and was considered a very good employee by the owners and well-liked by his co-workers. Some of them were Swedish like Gus, who had moved to the United States around 1866.

Work had been routine on that Saturday, October 23, 1886. Gus finished up around 5:00 p.m. and walked over to Gearhart Saloon on East State Street with a few of his friends from Trahern. He sat at the lunch counter and ordered a beer and one of the free lunches from the cook. He was enjoying his liver and rye bread when a commotion broke out in the back of the room. Later, witnesses would say that Gus ignored the fuss and continued with his food. Three men that were part of the tussle came over to Gus and harassed him about eating all the free food, but Gus continued to ignore them.

Gus finished his food and his beer, called out his compliments to the chef, said goodbye to his buddies and left the saloon to walk to his home on the corner of Fourth Street and Fifth Avenue. He knew his wife, Sophie, would be waiting with their three little children.

Suddenly, the three men from the bar were there in front of him, refusing to let him pass. Gus tried to push his way through, and the men jumped on him and threw him to the ground. He passed out when his head hit the sidewalk, but a twelve-year-old girl witnessed the attack. Olga Schaline would prove later to be a very good witness. She said that the three men threw Gus down and began to kick and choke him until they noticed her watching from across the street. The three men quickly escaped in the direction of Zion Lutheran Church.

Several men heard the commotion and ran to aid Gus as the attackers fled the scene. Gus was coherent and able to stand with help, though he complained of pain from the beating. He had several cuts on his face and was bleeding so much that even the men who knew him didn't recognize him at first.

By the next day, horrible bruises had formed on Gus's face, chest and ribs. His neck was so swollen from the choking that he couldn't speak above a whisper, and as the day progressed his breathing became labored. He seemed to realize early Monday morning that he would not recover. Gus became distressed and attempted to apologize to his wife, but she became very distraught and begged him not to leave her. Gus struggled to breathe until 4:00 a.m. on October 25. He was only forty-eight years old.

The autopsy would show that Gus had endured a horrible beating and was choked or kicked so savagely in the throat that the cartilage was fractured. The doctors who conducted his autopsy claimed they had never seen damage so severe.

The three men who attacked Gus were found very quickly. They went on trial for his death in the end of January 1887. Judge Brown believed them when they stated that they didn't mean to kill Gus but only to rough him up. During the sentencing, Judge Brown lectured them about the dangers of alcohol and their lack of comprehension of the damage that they had caused to the family. The attackers were all very young. David Creagan was only twenty years old, and he and John Laven, who was twenty-one, received ten-year sentences in Joliet. John Dixon, seventeen years old, reportedly took no part in the actual beating but acted as a lookout. He received a two-year sentence.

Sophie and her children moved from the house where Gus died. She stated that she could no longer live there without her husband. The house was rented out, but stories started to circulate that Gus's spirit was heard in the room where he died. The sound of a man wailing and sobbing came quite regularly. Neighbors reported strange noises that came from the house when no one was home. Though Sophie tried to rent the rooms, these stories frightened away prospective renters.

Other reports claimed that people would see a glowing light making its way through the house and sometimes a figure was seen to pull back the curtains from the window and peer out as if searching for someone. Neighbors were terrified by the look of sheer anguish on the face of the glowing specter.

People also spoke of seeing Gus's ghost wandering the area surrounding the intersection of Kishwaukee Street and Second Avenue, where the attack took place. Reports varied, but most stated that the ghost appeared to be so solid that you would not realize it was a spirit until the form turned and you could look at the face. People who had known him were horrified to recognize Gus.

The reports of the restless spirit of Gus Valentine continued in the newspapers for quite some time before fading away. Hopefully, Gus took comfort in the knowledge that the Trahern Company and the Zion Lutheran Church generously gathered donations to help Sophie and her children.

From author's collection.

Part II

LEGENDS, CURSES AND OTHER CURIOSITIES

There are no such things as curses; only people and their decisions
—*Yvonne Woon,* Dead Beautiful

22

THE PRINCESS OF BROWN'S HILL

The H.H. Hamilton family was well known in Rockford. Herbert was a very successful lawyer who had dealings in Minneapolis, Minnesota, as well as Rockford. Herbert lived his whole life in Winnebago County. He had a lucrative law office located on East State Street and also dealt in real estate in Minnesota. H.H. would eventually branch out to include raising racehorses. His horses were exceptional racers and did quite well. Businessmen who knew H.H. would say that he seemed to have the Midas touch when it came to business, and the papers of the day really emphasized it when he made his first million.

Carolyn Shoudy Hamilton became Herbert's wife on February 16, 1876. She was born in Rochelle and then moved to Rockford, where she grew up. Carolyn made a name for herself in Rockford by creating beautiful paintings and designing incredible gardens.

The Hamiltons had been blessed with a beautiful, charming daughter whom they named Barbara. She grew up to be a bright, well-behaved child who adored horses. Unfortunately, Barbara's love of horses would lead to a terrible accident. She fell while riding her favorite horse one day and it caused internal injuries.

Herbert used his considerable resources, and Barbara was seen by all the finest doctors. He also remodeled their home to make her bed rest more comfortable. The family even stayed in Chicago for a time while Barbara received treatments. Barbara struggled to regain her health. It must have frustrated this young family that, even with all their money, they were powerless to help their beloved daughter.

The H.H. Hamilton Home in Rockford. *From Midway Village Museum, Rockford.*

Barbara Hamilton was only fourteen years old when she died on June 6, 1909, in her home at 933 North Second Street. She took a turn for the worse, and her father was called home from his business in Minneapolis. He frantically made the journey to Janesville by train and the rest of the way by automobile. He got to her bedside just a few minutes before she passed away. Unfortunately, Barbara was unconscious, and her devastated father doubted whether she knew he was there.

Before her illness, Barbara spent time riding horses and was a member of the Children of the American Revolution. She was said to have been a very sweet young girl, and everyone who knew her loved her, especially her friends at Hall School. She was H.H. and Carolyn's only child, and they were inconsolable when she died.

Mr. Hamilton decided to have a mausoleum designed in memory of his daughter. He hired the R. Trigg Marble and Granite Company for the project. The front of the tomb faced Greenmount Avenue. A newspaper article from November 30, 1909, stated, "The entrance is plainly visible from the windows of the Hamilton home, two blocks to the north."

The walls of the mausoleum were granite that was brought all the way from the mountains of North Carolina. It stood nine feet deep and nine feet tall.

The inside had space for four coffins and was faced with Italian marble and ceiling to match. The floor was designed with polished granite. H.H. Hamilton even paid to have the mausoleum built into the hillside. The exterior entrance was landscaped and included decorative shrubbery. The whole mausoleum and landscaping cost over $8,000.

The Hamiltons grew apart after Barbara's death. They divorced, and Carolyn threw herself into her art. Besides creating her own artwork, she helped other artists. Carolyn was a charter member of the Rockford Art Association and hosted many artists at her home on North Second Street. Carolyn was also known for her garden designs. She was recognized for her designs of notable gardens all over northern Illinois. Carolyn died in 1939 in her home that she

The Hamilton Mausoleum at Cedar Bluff Cemetery. *From author's collection.*

shared with her sister-in-law, Mrs. Fred Shoudy. She was laid to rest in the mausoleum created by her former husband in honor of Barbara.

Herbert remarried in 1914 to Miss Elizabeth Sandidge in Minnesota. He passed away there in 1932.

There is a legend surrounding Barbara. She loved horses, and when her beloved horse passed away, rumor has it that the family buried it in the hillside so that it could be close to Barbara. Psychics visiting the area in Cedar Bluff have been confused and startled to see a horse running through the cemetery. Though the origin of this legend has been lost long ago, maybe it gave Barbara's loved ones some peace to imagine her buried there in the ornate mausoleum in the hill next to one of her favorite companions.

WHEN JESUS CAME TO WINNEBAGO COUNTY

George Jacob Schweinfurth was born in 1853 in Marion, Ohio. He had a typical childhood though his mother would later claim that she knew from the day he was born that God had a special plan for her son. That special plan would eventually involve hundreds of followers, numerous scandals and a six-hundred-acre farm named Mount Zion.

George would become involved with a religious movement started by a woman named Dorinda Beekman, the wife of a preacher. The Church Triumphant was originally based in Byron, Illinois, but Dorinda's claims soon had her followers ostracized from that community. George met Dorinda in December 1877, and they soon became kindred spirits.

George proved to be a gifted speaker. He was very handsome, and some would even claim that he looked just like Jesus Christ or what they imagined Jesus to look like at this time. Young, handsome and very persuasive were all words that were used to describe

Artist's sketch of George Jacob Schweinfurth. *From* Rockford Morning Star.

George back in the beginning. Young women were especially drawn to George, and he was very quickly ordained a bishop in the church.

Dorinda became sick and her congregation did all they could to cure her. Dorinda told them that this was a test and that she would surely rise again from her death bed if her followers prepared her body properly and had enough faith. The authorities heard of the vigils being held over Dorinda's body and forced the followers to bury the week-old body. That might have been the end of the Beekmanites and the Church Triumphant if George hadn't stepped forward to accept the role of leader.

George began to claim that he was the risen Messiah and that as such, he had unlimited powers. He could perform many miracles, including curing those afflicted with disease and even, just like Christ himself, raise people from the dead. When asked by a reporter if he really believed himself to be Christ, Schweinfurth replied, "I am more than that. I am the perfect man. I am God."

George drew more people into the faith and began to search for a place for the center of what was quickly becoming a religious movement. It was at this time that a loyal follower, Spencer Weldon, offered his lovely six-hundred-acre farm and home to George. In 1880, the Weldon family consisted of Spencer; his wife, Agnes Kelley; and their six children.

George gladly accepted the generous offer and mortgaged the Weldons' farm to expand the buildings and house to better fit the growing congregation. Whole families began to flock to the farm near the little town of Winnebago. George insisted that the families live apart. The men

The Weldon farm. *From author's collection.*

cared for the land and handled the livestock while the women worked in the house and tended the gardens. The farm grew very prosperous, and George eventually expanded into horse breeding. He proved to be a keen businessman and was soon raking in the profits. George's quarters inside the large farmhouse were expanded and made very luxurious.

Inevitably, the word began to spread about Heaven, as the congregation called it, and new followers came from all over the country. In order to live in Heaven, a person needed to surrender all of his or her worldly possessions to the church, which in turn took care of all the person's needs. Most men lived in dormitories in the barn, and the women stayed in the house with the prophet. Marriages were no longer acknowledged, and as one might imagine, this caused many conflicts.

The Church Triumphant numbers soon grew to several hundred. The social status of the majority of these people was surprising. These were not country bumpkins but highly educated, upper society people who included the wives of businessmen, lawyers and doctors who brought their husbands into the fold. When the men balked, the women left without them. Some of these women either forced their children to accompany them or deserted the entire family.

Certain young women who were very beautiful soon became the favorites of the self-proclaimed Messiah. One of these angels was the eldest daughter of the Weldons, Mary Louise. She was around twenty-five years old when the family home became known as Heaven. She was very beautiful and one of George's most devout followers.

One of the fundamental beliefs of the Church Triumphant was the immaculate conception of Mary with the child of the Holy Spirit. It was such a vital part of their belief that when certain angels became pregnant, followers all believed that they, like the Virgin Mary, carried the children of God. Though the exact number of these children has been lost, at least four were born in Heaven. Two children were born to the head angel, Aurora Tuttle; one to Mary Teft; and one to Mary Weldon.

Needless to say, this caused quite a controversy, and newspaper reporters soon flocked to the farm. The stories spread until they were reported nationwide. When one of the reporters asked Spencer Weldon what he thought about his daughter becoming pregnant, he replied that he was overjoyed that she carried the child of God.

The controversy continued, and charges were brought against the three angels and George for immoral behavior. In order to quiet some of the rumors, George married Aurora in the late 1890s, though this proved to be a case of too little, too late. Finally, in 1900, George left Heaven behind and brought Aurora and their two children to Rockford before changing his name to Furth. The man who was once considered by so many to be Jesus himself moved to Chicago and became a realtor. He died there in 1915 still shrouded in scandal and controversy.

24

THE VENGEANCE OF CHIEF BIG THUNDER

Northern Illinois was once inhabited by the Native American tribe known as the Potawatomi. The major chief for this area was Chief Big Thunder, supposedly named for the sound of his thundering voice. Before he passed away, he requested to be placed facing the West. Big Thunder foretold of a great battle between his tribe and another. He told his people that when the time came for this battle, he would come back and lead them to victory. Big Thunder died sometime around 1800, and his people placed

The plaque for Chief Big Thunder. *From author's collection.*

him on a bench on the highest spot around and surrounded his body with a fence. They gave him offerings of food and his favorite tobacco. Though the battle he foresaw never happened and Big Thunder never rose from the dead, his people continued to honor him by placing tobacco in his lap as an offering.

During the early 1800s, Big Thunder's burial place was on the main stagecoach trail between Chicago and Galena, and his grave and body soon became victims to relic hunters. These white men and women took the chief's bones and placed them on display in their homes or businesses. The people of the area considered Big Thunder a tourist attraction of sorts, and when actual relics became scarce, they replaced the chief's bones with pig bones to continue to draw people to the sight. Big Thunder's Skull was supposedly removed by Josiah Goodhue, who then donated it to the Rush Medical College. The skull was reported lost during the great fire of 1871.

Artist's sketch of Josiah Goodhue. *From* Daily Register Gazette.

Dr. Goodhue was well known in Rockford. Josiah was born in Putney, Vermont, in 1803 and moved his family here from Chicago in 1838. He graduated from the Yale School of Medicine and then started a practice in St. Thomas in Upper Canada. It was here that he met his wife, Catherine Dunn. They had thirteen children, five of whom died before reaching the age of five.

Dr. Josiah Goodhue had many achievements to his name by the time he reached Rockford; he was instrumental in organizing the Rush Medical College and served on the first board of trustees. He also designed the first city seal for Chicago.

The townspeople of Rockford remember Josiah today for his work as a doctor and for changing the name of the city to Rockford from Midway, as it was previously known.

Unfortunately, Josiah is best known for his demise, which was said to be the result of a curse by Big Thunder's tribe. The Potawatomi tribe heard of the desecration of their beloved chief's final resting place and swore revenge against anyone who had taken his bones, especially the man who had stolen his skull.

Josiah Goodhue's grave at Cedar Bluff Cemetery. *From author's collection.*

On December 31, 1847, Josiah, then just forty-four years old, was attending to a patient at the house of Richard Styles about four miles west of the city on State Road. When he was finished treating his patient, he decided to walk a neighbor woman, Mrs. Stoughton, to her house. It was dark, and though he was warned by Mrs. Stoughton about the danger, Josiah fell headfirst into a freshly dug well. He was rescued but died shortly thereafter.

The stories of the curse of Big Thunder escalated after Josiah's death. Many insisted that Big Thunder had finally received his revenge. The city of Belvidere honored Chief Big Thunder by placing a rock with a plaque at his final resting place, in front of the courthouse.

One other thing that Josiah left the city of Rockford was the cemetery that he fondly named Cedar Bend, which later became Cedar Bluff Cemetery. He was buried there on the top of a small hill with his family and a view of the city he loved.

25

THE WITCH OF McGREGOR ROAD

This local legend has been around for years. Some people say it started circulating in the 1980s while others put the origin even further back. Researching local legends is always a challenge, and attempts to find the origins of Beulah the Witch story proved nearly impossible. There is a story that took place in 1913 that may have been where the story began.

In 1913, there was a *Register Republic* article that spoke of a family that was having some problems. This family of L.J. Johnson lived on a farm located four miles outside Rockford. A report was called into the police about a terrible fight that occurred in the home. The caller went on to say that one of the daughters was being attacked with a hammer. The police hurried to the Johnson home to find the six members fighting with one another.

The family members, with the exception of the father, believed that they suffered from horrible headaches and other physical ailments, all caused by one of the daughters, Beulah Andrews. The Johnson household was in constant turmoil because Mr. Johnson took Beulah's side while everyone else believed her to be a witch. The verbal altercation grew so heated that one of the daughters had a seizure, causing the women to become even more excited.

The police became concerned by the probability of violence between the family members and finally decided that something more needed to be done. The entire family was loaded into the police wagon and driven to the jail. On the ride, all of the members, except for Mr. Johnson and Beulah, complained of attacks brought on them by the witch.

The neighbors described the breakdown of the family and the horrible shouting matches that occurred on a daily basis. They also informed the police that the Johnsons already had one daughter who had been committed to the state hospital for the mentally insane. Another daughter had been in and out of Elgin with mental issues, though the neighbors weren't clear on that daughter's identity. The neighbors also spoke of the family's belief that Beulah was a witch and caused much mental anguish for the family members. When asked, the neighbors couldn't say if they believed the family's claims about Beulah. But they did point out that Beulah and the father, Mr. Johnson, were seen in the woods with lanterns late at night.

The Johnson family was taken to the police station to be escorted to court in front of Judge Louison. The judge listened as the family testified against one another. They told of one daughter's descent into madness that led to her placement into the state hospital for the insane. Mrs. Johnson claimed that her daughter Beulah would cause her and the other family members to have horrible headaches. They were also made to dance uncontrollably.

Beulah, the accused daughter, denied practicing witchcraft. She also stated that she was too busy helping her father to raise the vegetables that they sold from their truck. "I have no time to do all those things," Beulah testified.

Mr. Johnson had tears in his eyes as the judge rendered his decision for the family to split up. Beulah returned to the family farm with her father while Mrs. Johnson and Marguerite were ordered to live with Mrs. Johnson's sister.

Whether this story was later recalled to add fuel to the fire for the Beulah legend is unclear. There appears to be no connection between the Johnson family and the woman who would suffer from the harassment in the future. Over the years, the Beulah the Witch story changed until there were several different versions.

One version of the story claimed that there was an old witch named Beulah who lived in a house in some secluded woods on McGregor Road. She was allegedly responsible for abducting children to use in her satanic practices. Instead of deterring teenagers from going to the woman's house, this story had the opposite effect. They flocked to the area around her house.

Another version claimed that this woman had been a teacher in a one-room schoolhouse located on McGregor Road. While Beulah was teaching one day, the building caught fire, and two of her students died. Beulah was so devastated by the fire that she purchased the school and turned it into her home. The parents of the children she taught held her responsible for the deaths and ostracized Beulah. The guilt she felt and the treatment by the locals pushed her over the edge into insanity. She was seen wandering the woods around her house, calling to the children who were lost in the fire. Beulah was sometimes accompanied by her two large German shepherds, one white and one black.

No matter the version heard, the stories always caused the same reaction and gave locals a reason to drive by Beulah's house at all hours of the night and day. These visitors would throw items into her yard and beep their horns in an attempt to get a glimpse of the witch.

There is no way to validate these stories, of course. But there was an article, however, about two men who were arrested for harassing a retired schoolteacher who lived on McGregor and Weldon Roads. The 1973 article listed the elderly woman's name as Marie Buskie, and further research confirmed this as the identity of the woman who lived at the address listed on McGregor Road.

Marie Buskie was born on May 7, 1907, to parents Richard and Augusta Buskie. There would be two boys and three girls born into the family. Marie was active in several clubs in high school and participated on the swim team. She showed interest in working with children as a teacher very early. The family was very involved in the Calvary Lutheran Church, and Marie, like her sisters, would teach Sunday school there.

Marie and her sisters also appeared to be quite daring. In a newspaper article dated 1925, Marie and her sister Lulu were attending college courses in DeKalb when the girls and their roommates decided to walk home to Rockford. The roommates gave up after only a few miles, but the other girls made it all the way to Rockford. They accepted a few rides from kind motorists, but the girls estimated they walked over twenty-two miles. It took them five and a half hours to get home. The sisters decided to take the train back down to school, claiming that they had already obtained a good deal of their gym credits for the year.

Marie taught in several Rockford schools after obtaining her degree, including Highland and Kishwaukee schools. She also continued her work with children through her church and during summers at supervised playgrounds.

Unlike her siblings, who all married, Marie lived with her parents on Prairie Road until their deaths. Her mother died in 1949 and her father in 1958. Sometime in the early 1960s, she moved into the house on McGregor Road. Though Marie dedicated her life to children, she never had any of her own. Marie was seventy-eight years old when she died on March 31, 1986, in Amberwood Care Center on Rockton Avenue.

The legend of Beulah the Witch will, no doubt, continue. The real mystery might just be why this elderly woman, who spent her life caring for children, would become the target of such maliciousness in the first place and why this story would continue for decades.

JAMES HENRY BREASTED

THE REAL "INDIANA JONES"?

James Henry Breasted was many things to many people, but most would agree that he seemed to be just plain lucky. He had a special knack for being in the right place at the right time.

James's grandfather Thomas Garrison moved his family from New Jersey to Rockford in 1853. He was in real estate, so he purchased land and built a beautiful home near the present-day John Street and Ridge Avenue area. Rockford has always been filled with beautiful homes, but from all descriptions, the house built by Thomas Garrison was exceptional. It supposedly cost around $24,000 in 1858, a very large sum for that time. Unfortunately, the beautiful house was completely consumed by a fire in 1868. The next house built by the family was much less grand but still a fine house. The Garrison home would be the center of the social life of Rockford due in part to Thomas's daughter, Harriet, who was involved with many activities.

Charles Breasted, James's father, was born in New York in 1832. He moved to Rockford in 1853 and became a partner with Israel Sovereign in the hardware business. They opened a hardware store, Breasted and Sovereign Hardware, on South Main Street between State and Elm Streets in the building that would later become the Chick House.

James Henry Breasted was born in Rockford on August 7, 1865, a son of Charles and Harriet. The family lived on Grant Street when James was a child. He attended Mrs. Squire's grade school shortly after the Civil War, and it was here that Breasted first uncovered his love of history. James, according to newspaper articles, spent time daydreaming of distant lands that he read about in books from the local library. He would sit watching the waters of the Rock River and imagine traveling to the places he read about.

When James was eight, the family moved to Downers Grove, Illinois, but they continued to return regularly to Rockford to visit his aunt Backus. Later, he would return to visit his parents' graves in Greenwood Cemetery. They both passed away in Chicago—Charles died in 1896 and Harriet in 1921.

James may have dreamed of faraway lands, but when he was planning a life for himself, his first choice was a little more down to earth. He planned to be a pharmacist but then changed his mind and decided to be a preacher. He attended Northwestern University (known now as North Central) in Naperville, Illinois. While he was attending the school for ministry, he discovered his love of languages. James decided to change schools, this time enrolling at Yale, where good timing played a part in his future. It was while James was attending Yale that he met William Rainey Harper, who really encouraged James to attend the University of Berlin to study Hebrew. This decision would open many doors later in his life.

James graduated from the University of Berlin with honors in 1894. While he was studying in Berlin, he met the lovely Frances Hart. Again, fate smiled on James, and he married Frances in Berlin before returning to Chicago.

James's old teacher, William Rainey Harper, would assist him when he became director of the University of Chicago and invited James to become a professor at the school. James worked very hard and spent years teaching, traveling and lecturing. He would eventually become the very first professor of Egyptology and Eastern history for any American university.

By 1899, James was already making a name for himself as one of the best-known archaeologists in the United States. In an article in the local newspaper, it stated, "Quite an interesting list of honors for a Rockford boy and we are not a bit ashamed of him."

James was not content to work just in the classroom. According to the *Hyde Park Herald*, "He dodged snipers, negotiated with sheiks, and uncovered some of the world's great art treasures on his trip to the war ravaged Middle East in 1919 and 1920." Breasted was joined by John D. Rockefeller Jr. to create the Oriental Institute of the University of Chicago. Breasted authored many books on the topics of archaeology, Eastern history and languages. His books are still quoted today. On a trip to the Middle East, James was able to purchase valuable pieces for the Oriental Institute right before the region changed its policy to discontinue large sales of antiquities.

There is a rumor that the famous Harrison Ford role of Indiana Jones was based on Rockford's very own James Henry Breasted. Even if the rumor is false, that is exactly the kind of man that James was, always ready for the next adventure.

James's luck held again when he was in the area of the Nile working on a project for the Oriental Institute. Howard Carter discovered King Tut's tomb and summoned James to the tomb to help decipher some of the royal seals. He was one of the first to enter the tomb of the boy king.

His translation of the hieroglyphs found on the walls confirmed the identity of the boy king, and his work in the tomb led Howard Carter to discover Tutankhamun's mummy. James supposedly stayed two long weeks down in the tomb and even slept in the chambers until the priceless items could be secured. His close association with this discovery would lead to rumors of a curse later.

James was very successful in his professional life, but unlike other adventurers of his day, James did not travel alone. Frances, James's wife, would accompany her husband on most of his expeditions, penetrating many remote parts of the world. She set up housekeeping on the Nile, was by his side when they were almost killed in a rafting expedition and assisted him when he traveled to the ruins of Persopolis in Persia. The couple had three children: Charles, James Jr. and a daughter, Astrid. Frances shared his triumphs and tragedies and did it all without much acknowledgement.

James would also discover the stables of King Solomon at Armageddon and King Sargon's temples in Assyria. Later, he would uncover the palace grounds of Alexander the Great. He did this all while maintaining his association with the Oriental Institute for forty years.

Breasted would give wonderful presentations, sharing photos of the places he had visited. One such trip involved the Temple of the Sun by Ramses II. People in the audience stated that they were transported to those far-off places. James could turn back time in his presentations until those locations, now buried in sand, seemed to rise shining and new before the audience. James also sprinkled his near-death experiences in the talks, leaving his audience thrilled with tales of barely escaping death at the hands of natives or thrilling raft rides over rapids.

It would irritate James that the most common question asked after one of these lectures was about the curse of King Tut's tomb. The curse stemmed from the words etched on the entrance to Tut's tomb, "Death shall come on swift wings to him that toucheth the tomb of the Pharaoh." The rumors spread that many people who entered the tomb would later die an early death. Since James's wife, Frances, had also spent time in the tomb, she, too, supposedly became a victim of the curse when she passed away in 1934.

The first to die was the man who financed Howard Carter's expeditions, Lord George Herbert, the Earl of Carnarvon. He died on March 25, 1923, and as the tale states, all of the lights went out in Cairo at the exact time of his death. His favorite dog, Susie, back home at his estate in England, gave a sharp howl and dropped dead at the same time that Carnarvon drew his last breath.

Lord Carnarvon was not in the best of health even before arriving in Egypt. He also received a very nasty mosquito bite that he nicked while shaving that later caused a bad infection that entered his blood. Lord Carnarvon's mysterious death caught the attention of Sir Arthur Conan Doyle, who helped spread the "curse" rumors. Some say that the origins of the curse might have stemmed from Howard Carter himself. He feared that the treasures he found would be stolen and knew that the slaves might talk. He supposedly started the rumor to discourage the superstitious men from breaking in and stealing the priceless items. Howard Carter would not have been the first to suggest a cursed mummy killing those who dare to desecrate the tombs of royals. The first ghost story about a mummy was published in 1699.

Later, the claims would spread from those who entered the tomb to include anyone who touched an item from the tomb. No matter who started it, Carter and Breasted quickly grew frustrated with the subject. Even though James called the curse tommyrot, the rumors continued long after both Howard Carter and James Henry Breasted were gone. The last story of a death allegedly caused by the curse took place in the 1970s, when a maintenance man died while unpacking an exhibit of the items from King Tut's tomb in London. The museum supposedly covered up the death for over twenty years in order to dispel the rumors the death would cause.

James's wife, Frances, died in July 1934 after a very exciting life traveling to different countries and helping her husband and children fulfill their dreams. James would remarry when he was sixty-nine. His new bride, Imogene, was the sister of his first wife and was fifty when they wed.

Breasted became ill during the couple's honeymoon trip to Egypt. He died traveling home to New York City in December 1935. His ashes were brought to Greenwood Cemetery so that he could be buried next to his parents. In a biography of his father, James's son Charles wrote, "His visits always included a quiet hour in the Greenwood Cemetery beside the grave of his parents. He seemed to derive strength and inspiration from contemplating their peaceful sleep, and comfort from knowing that when his longest journey was ended, he would lie beside them." Later a slab of stone from the Valley of the Kings would be sent by the Egyptian government in memory of all James had done for its country. James's death led people to speculate whether he was part of the curse placed on anyone who dared to enter the tomb despite the fact that he was seventy years old when he died. James was so worried that people would blame the curse that he arranged for the *New York Times* to post statements from three different doctors that his death was from natural causes and not because of King Tut's curse. The papers did this, but they all mentioned that Breasted was the seventh person to die of the twenty-two who originally entered the tomb.

James Henry Breasted's story still intrigues people today, nearly eighty years after his death. People are still fascinated by the thrilling tales of his adventures, the possibility of a royal mummy's curse and the story of this hometown Rockford boy whose fate became so closely connected with a boy king from thousands of years ago.

BIBLIOGRAPHY

The research for these stories has taken place over ten years. Since the primary source of information was local news accounts, there will obviously be some incomplete information. Every attempt has been made to corroborate with different sources.

INTRODUCTION

Church, Charles. *History of Rockford and Winnebago County, Illinois.* Rockford, IL: W.P. Lamb, 1900.

CHAPTER 1

Rockford (IL) Morning Star. "Girl, 4, Sees Father Fire Pistol Shots." January 18, 1958.
———. "Inquest Announced in Murder Suicide." January 18, 1958.
Rockford (IL) Register Star. "Divorce Suits Filed." January 15, 1958.
———. "Mrs. Geraldine Bourbon Filed for Divorce." December 29, 1957.
Rockford (IL) Republic. "Kills Wife, Self." January 17, 1958.
———. "Man, 31, Slays Wife Kills Self." January 17, 1958.
———. "Police Look for Slayers' Car." January 24, 1958.

CHAPTER 2

May, Maureen Mall. Interview with the author, 2013.

Rockford (IL) Morning Star. "Fair Rockford Girl Is a Bride." May 22, 1902.

———. "Mrs. Amy Barnes Lane." August 18, 1959.

———. "Mrs. W.F. Barnes Is Summoned to Eternal Rest." May 18, 1922.

———. "Rockford Represented." January 13, 1894.

———. "Wins a Southern Bride." February 4, 1912.

Rockford (IL) Register Republic. "Barnes Dinner Is Tonight." January 24, 1912.

———. "Celebrate Golden Wedding." January 10, 1921.

———. "The Change in the Shops of W.F. and John Barnes." July 12, 1906

———. "Children Benefit by W.F. Barnes Will." January 1, 1931.

———. "Her Eyesight Will Be Saved." September 18, 1902.

———. "Mrs. Barnes Book." February 25, 1903.

———. "Mrs. William F. Barnes." May 16, 1922.

———. "1911 Racer Risked Life, Inheritance." August 22, 1964.

Rockford (IL) Register Star. "Forest View Abbey's Demise." September 5, 1984.

———. "Mrs. Barnes Reception." January 15, 1912.

CHAPTER 3

May, Maureen Mall. Interview with the author, 2013.

Rockford (IL) Daily Gazette. "Social Rockford Gathers to Pay Tribute to the Bride and Groom." May 29, 1889.

Rockford (IL) Daily Register. "It Will Be a Tug." February 4, 1890.

Rockford (IL) Morning Star. "Burpee Art Museum Will Be Scene of a Final Large Social Function." December 6, 1935.

———. "A Noble Spirit Is Stilled." November 17, 1897.

———. "Rockford Inventor, Manny Helped Lincoln Win a War." February 8, 1953.

Rockford (IL) Republic. "Death of Mrs. John P. Manny." December 27, 1909.

Rockford (IL) Weekly Gazette. "First Report for the John P. Manny." June 21, 1882.

———. "Rockford, Illinois." August 6, 1868.

CHAPTER 4

Emporia (KS) Emporia Gazette. "Death of Camp Commandant Colonel Hagadorn Found Dead in His Quarters at Camp Grant This Morning—May Have Been Suicide." October 8, 1918.

Rockford (IL) Gazette. "Bullet Wound Head." October 8, 1918.

Rockford (IL) Republic. "New Commandant to Take Hold Tomorrow." September 6, 1918.

Weisensel, Yolanda. Interview with the author, September 2012.

CHAPTER 5

Author interview with anonymous source, September 2012.

Weisensel, Yolanda. Interview with the author, September 2012.

CHAPTER 6

Mangas, Marty. Interview with the author, September 2006.

Rockford (IL) Morning Star. "Coronado." February 13, 1977.

———. "Gene Tierney's Rockford Visit Definitely Booked." September 4, 1942.

———. "Louis St. Pierre to Retire from Theater." February 29, 1948

———. "New Hospital Unit Serves Varied Needs." October 11, 1975.

———. "Piano Company Founder Dies." December 16, 1939.

———. "Simple Home Wedding." January 27, 1911.

———. "369,100 E Bond House to Hear Radio Forum." June 16, 1944.

Rockford (IL) Register Star. "Coronado Shaped a Generation." January 16, 2001.

———. "Fountain of History." November 13, 1995.

Rockford (IL) Republic. "Erma Van Matre Obituary." March 19, 1969.

———. "Group Pledges $250,000 to Hospital." August 23, 1974.

———. "Theater Chain Founder Dies," April 24, 1953

———. "355 Camp Grant Chosen Officer's Camp." May 13, 1918.

———. "Willard Van Matre." April 25, 1953.

Chapter 7

Rockford (IL) Daily Gazette. "Chair in Which Roosevelt Sat." June 4, 1903.

Rockford (IL) Morning Star. "Funeral of A.F. Stevens Held Yesterday at Memorial Hall." February 22, 1908.

———. "Grand Army at Durand Grave of Comrade." April 19, 1914.

Rockford (IL) Register Star. "War Memorial Fund and Hall Create Rift." June 25, 1984.

Rockford (IL) Republic. "Soldiers' and Sailors' Memorial Hall Dedication Program." June 2, 1903.

Chapter 8

Litteral, Steve. Interview with the author, September 2007.

Rockford (IL) Daily Gazette. "The Tinker Monument." May 14, 1902.

Rockford (IL) Morning Star. "Robert Hall Tinker Dies Here." January 1, 1925.

Rockford (IL) Register Star. "Holiday Entries from Tinker's Historic Diaries." December 5, 1997.

———. "Readers Share Family Histories." December 9, 2002.

———. "The Rebirth of Tinker Swiss Cottage." May 27, 2005.

———. "Tinker a Place for People." November 22, 1981.

Chapter 9

Rockford (IL) Daily Gazette. "Olin Brouse Died This Morning." August 20, 1921.

———. "$3,00 Given to W.M. Kimball." October 1, 1906.

Rockford (IL) Morning Star. "Her Song Won Him." January 30, 1891.

———. "Is Disinherited." May 25, 1895.

———. "It Was Successful in Every Respect." November 5, 1893.

———. "Olin Brouse Dies Suddenly." August 21, 1921.

———. "Renounced the Will." July 16, 1895.

Rockford (IL) *Republic.* "Mrs. C.M. Utter Passes Away." September 1, 1906.

———. "Olin Brouse Dies Suddenly at Home." August 20, 1921.

Tietz, Mark. Interview with the author, 2010.

Chapter 10

Rockford (IL) Daily Gazette. "Dr. George Haskell." December 16, 1904
Rockford (IL) Morning Star. "Ghosts Visit Haskell Park." June 13, 1902.
———. "A Life of Sorrow." July 20, 1896.
———. "May Hang in June." May 16, 1897.
Rockford (IL) Republic. "Paid the Penalty." June 11, 1897.

Chapter 11

Lewandowski, Sue. Interview with the author, August 2012.
Rockford (IL) Register Star. "Preserving Heritage." May 7, 1989.

Chapter 12

Rockford (IL) Morning Star. "Mrs. Emma P. Jones." February 11, 1964.
———. "Ray E. Jones." December 30, 1962.
Rockford (IL) Register Star. "Changing Haunts: Architects Wonder If the Spirit Is Moving." February 15, 1988.
Rockford (IL) Republic. "Ghost Stories Add to the Holiday Spirit." October 31, 1988.
———. "Transfer Firm President Dies." December 30, 1940.

Chapter 13

Rockford (IL) Morning Star. "How Things Have Changed." November 3, 1974.
Rockford (IL) Register Star. "Anthony V. 'Tony' Salamone." November 23, 2000.
Rockford (IL) Republic. "Local Airlift to Enhance GOP Breakfast." February 25, 1969.
———. "Miss Schoening Engaged to Wed 'Tony' Salamone." June 8, 1944.

Chapter 14

Rockford (IL) Morning Star. "Bertha Ritter, Fred Goetz Exchange Vows."
February 15, 1948.
———. "Fred Goetz Rathskeller Founder Dies." November 21, 1976.
———. "Restaurateur's Wife Is First 1947 Auto Fatality." January 3, 1947.
———. "Rockford Fred Goetz Is Alive and Well." March 23, 1934.
———. "Travelers and Collegians in News Today." June 17, 1947.
Rockford (IL) Republic. "Ray Goetz Nominated for Law School Honor."
January 19, 1949.

Chapter 15

Rockford (IL) Morning Star. "That Queer Light Seen Every Night." June 3, 1891.

Chapter 16

Rockford (IL) Daily Gazette. "Had Ghost Dance." July 29, 1896.
Rockford (IL) Republic. "Looking for Ghosts." July 29, 1896.

Chapter 17

Rockford (IL) Daily Gazette. "Ghosts at the Gas House." April 6, 1893.

Chapter 18

Rockford (IL) Daily Gazette. "Days Doing at Belvidere." June 30, 1904.
Rockford (IL) Morning Star. "Chief Theorizes Faulty Wiring Triggered Fire."
December 22, 1972.
Rockford (IL) Register Star. "Belvidere Couple Killed in Collision." February
18, 1979.

———. "Blood's Point." November 12, 2004.

———. "Boone County Facts." November 11, 1996.

———. "Driver Dies from Auto Accident Injuries." October 10, 1995.

———. "Pat's Stuff." December 17, 2003.

———. "Roads Less Taken: The Country Drive." March 22, 2001.

CHAPTER 19

Madison (WI) Weekly Wisconsin Patriot. "Items Pertaining to the Massacre of Col. Ellsworth." June 1, 1861.

Rockford (IL) Daily Gazette. "C.H. Spafford Dies Suddenly." January 4, 1908.

Rockford (IL) Morning Star. "Col. Ellsworth Shares Billing with Lincoln in Exhibit at Webster House in Elkhorn, Wis." August 16, 1959.

———. "Historic Gregory House Leaves Rich Tradition." November 25, 1956.

———. "An Old and Honored Resident." September 10, 1892.

Rockford (IL) Republic. "Carrie S. Brett Is No More." October 9, 1911.

———. "Old Settler Is Dead." July 19, 1901.

———. "Rockford, Nation Mourned Over Death of Dashing Colonel." May 28, 1960.

Rockford (IL) Weekly Gazette. "Col. Ellsworth's Presentiment of an Early Death." June 8, 1861.

CHAPTER 20

Rockford (IL) Register Star. "The Demon Within." March 22, 1982.

———. "Eerie Presence Unnerves Family." February 24, 1982.

———. "Family Never Sought Publicity." March 22, 1982.

———. "What Lurks in the Household?" February 21, 1982.

CHAPTER 21

Rockford (IL) Daily Gazette. "All in Jail." October 26, 1886.

———. "Foul Murder." October 25, 1886.

———. "Skandinaver." October 26,1886.

Rockford (IL) Weekly Gazette. "Friday." November 3, 1886.

———. "Result of Coroner's Inquest." October 27, 1886.

CHAPTER 22

Rockford (IL) Daily Gazette. "Death Visits the Hamilton Home," June 5, 1909.

———. "Mausoleum is Complete." November 30, 1909.

Rockford (IL) Morning Star. "Death Claims Mrs. Hamilton." November 22, 1939.

———. "Miss Hamilton Dead." June 6, 1909.

Rockford (IL) Republic. "Bert Hamilton Is a Millionaire." July 1, 1911.

CHAPTER 23

Rockford (IL) Daily Gazette. "Cases to Be Dropped." September 10, 1896.

———. "Col. Jake to Marry." September 8, 1896.

———. "Funeral in Heaven." September 12, 1895.

———. "The New Messiah?" August 14, 1890.

———. "Schweinfurth Invited to Quit Rockford Vicinage." December 12, 1900.

———. "Schweinfurth Must Go." August 13, 1890.

———. "Why Schweinfurth Dissolved His Rockford 'Heaven.'" September 27, 1910.

Rockford (IL) Morning Star. "Disagrees with Helen Gardner." January 24, 1893.

———. "A Fallen Christ." August 5, 1890.

———. "He Escapes the Jail." April 28, 1896.

———. "He Is Safe in His Haven." April 8, 1891.

———. "One More Peter Becomes a Betrayer." August 30, 1891.

———. "Ran Away from Heaven." September 15, 1899.

———. "Rise and Fall of Schweinfurth." June 27, 1897.

———. "The Sad Story of Lilly Beekman." May 31, 1892.

———. "Scotch View of Him." July 25, 1897.

Rockford (IL) Republic. "Bogus Christ to Wed." September 18, 1896.

———. "G.J. Schweinfurth Goes." July 15, 1899.

———. "'Heaven' Organized." November 9, 1897.

———. "Heaven to Be Moved." July 24, 1896.

———. "Schweinfurth's Sensational Career at Weldon." September 26, 1910.

———. "Tears Off His Mask." July 31, 1896.

———. "To Be Four Weddings." August 4, 1896.

CHAPTER 24

Rockford (IL) Daily Gazette. "Man Who Named the Town." December 16, 1904.

———. "The Story of Dr. Josiah Goodhue Who Gave Rockford Its Name." May 17, 1904.

Rockford (IL) Forum. "Estate of Josiah C. Goodhue Dec'd." May 3, 1848.

Rockford (IL) Morning Star. "County's Medical History Traced to First Physician in Belvidere." May 6, 1945.

———. "Crime Came Back to Haunt Him." October 31, 1976.

———. "Mrs. Barnum, Last Goodhue Died Tuesday." December 9, 1925.

Rockford (IL) Republic. "Big Thunder's Skull." March 30, 1933.

———. "How Rockford Got Its Name." May 21, 1948.

———. "Physicians Prominent in History of County." September 4, 1950

CHAPTER 25

Rockford (IL) Morning Star. "Mother Labels Daughter a Witch." July 17, 1913.

Rockford (IL) Republic. "Big Fight in Home Near Rockford." July 17, 1913.

———. "Broke Up Home Where Witch Held Sway." July 18, 1913.

———. "Bully-Boy Youths Harass Old Woman." September 14, 1973.

CHAPTER 26

Rockford (IL) Daily Gazette. "Dr. Breasted Talks." April 14, 1896.

———. "John D. Picks Local Man to Head Museum." February 19, 1926.

————. "Mrs. Breasted Dead at 85; Burial Here." November 21, 1921.

————. "Rockford Man to Describe Tut's Tomb." November 13, 1923.

Rockford (IL) Morning Star. "Breasted Dies of Infection." December 3, 1935.

————. "Breasted Told Story of King Cheop's Tomb." April 27, 1918.

————. "Ex-Local Man Dedicates New Institute." December 6, 1931.

————. "Former Rockford Boy Who Has Gained Fame." March 23, 1902.

————. "Granite from Ancient Egypt to Mark Breasted's Burial Place." January 19, 1938.

————. "James H. Breasted to Nile Region." October 21, 1906.

————. "Marries First Wife's Sister." June 8, 1935.

————. "Pioneer of the Past." April 14, 1943.

Rockford (IL) Register Star. "City's "Pioneer of the Past' Honored." September 11, 1983.

Rockford (IL) Republic. "Breasted's Dream." April 28, 1930.

————. "Dr. Breasted Loved Rockford." December 4, 1935.

————. "Famous City Native Remembered in Ceremony." December 2, 1975.

————. "Former Rockford Man Speaks to Woman's Club." February 14, 1912.

————. "Forty Interesting Years." July 17, 1934.

————. "Made a Name for Himself." November 10, 1898.

————. "Roads of Destiny." October 10, 1929.

About the Author

Kathi Kresol has been researching Rockford's history for the past ten years. She shares the fascinating stories she uncovers through her website, www.hauntedrockford. com; her "Voices from the Grave" column in the *Rock River Times* weekly newspaper; and her Haunted Rockford Tours. Kathi's obsession is history, and she loves the opportunity to

Photograph by Aryn Kresol.

share this passion through the stories she collects. Kathi is a member of the Rockford Historical Society, has worked at the Rockford Public Library for years and loves sharing her enthusiasm for history and reading in any way possible. Along with researching and writing about history, Kathi has given presentations on true crime cases, paranormal encounters and Rockford history. She has also been interviewed for several radio shows, local newscasts and newspapers and always considers it an honor to share the stories of the men, women and children who have called Rockford home.